Home-Tested
SLOW
COOKER
Recipes

Publications International, Ltd.

Photography on pages 7, 9, 11, 13, 17, 19, 21, 23, 25, 27, 29, 31, 33, 35, 37, 39, 49, 51,
53, 55, 73, 75, 79, 81, 83, 85, 89, 93, 95, 101, 105, 129, 137, 143, 151, 153, 157, 161,
173 and 185 by Stephen Hamilton Photographics, Inc.

Photographers: Stephen Hamilton, Tate Hunt
Photographers' Assistant: Tom Gajda
Prop Stylist: Paula Walters
Food Stylists: Christianne Ingegno, Susie Skoog
Assistant Food Stylist: Lisa Knych

Pictured on the front cover: French Country Slow Cooker Chicken *(page 84),* submitted
by Teri Lindquist (inset photo).

Pictured on the back cover *(left to right):* Easy Family Burritos *(page 6)* and
1-2-3-4 Chili *(page 150).*

ISBN: 0-7853-7993-2

Library of Congress Control Number: 2002109071

Manufactured in China.

8 7 6 5 4 3 2 1

Microwave Cooking: Microwave ovens vary in wattage. Use the cooking times as
guidelines and check for doneness before adding more time.

Preparation/Cooking Times: Preparation times are based on the approximate amount
of time required to assemble the recipe before cooking, baking, chilling or serving.
These times include preparation steps such as measuring, chopping and mixing. The
fact that some preparations and cooking can be done simultaneously is taken into
account. Preparation of optional ingredients and serving suggestions is not included.

CONTENTS

THE SLOW COOKER:

First introduced in the 1970's, the slow cooker is making a comeback. Considering the hectic pace of today's lifestyles, it's no wonder so many people have rediscovered this time-saving kitchen helper. All you have to do is spend a few minutes preparing the ingredients, and then let your slow cooker do the rest. In 10, 8, or as few as 4 hours, a hot, delicious meal will be ready to serve!

HELPFUL HINTS:

- Manufacturers recommend slow cookers be one-half to three-quarters full for best results.

- Keep a lid on it! The slow cooker can take as long as twenty minutes to regain heat lost when the cover is removed. If a recipe calls for stirring or checking the dish near the end of its cooking time, replace the lid as quickly as you can.

- Follow the manufacturer's instructions for cleaning your slow cooker. To make cleanup even easier, spray the inside with nonstick cooking spray before adding the ingredients.

- Always taste the finished dish before serving, and adjust seasonings to your preference.

FOOD SAFETY TIPS:

Once a dish is cooked, don't keep it in the slow cooker too long. Foods need to be kept cooler than 40°F or hotter than 140°F to avoid the growth of harmful bacteria. Remove the food to a clean container, and cover and refrigerate it as soon as possible. Do not reheat leftovers in the slow cooker. Instead, use your microwave oven, range-top or oven.

ADAPTING RECIPES

If you'd like to adapt a favorite recipe to your slow cooker, follow these simple guidelines. First, try to find a similar slow cooker recipe in this book or in your manufacturer's guide. Note the cooking times, liquid, quantity and size of meat and vegetable pieces. Because the slow cooker captures moisture, you will want to reduce the amount of liquid, often by as much as half. Add dairy products toward the end of the cooking time, since they tend to curdle. The following chart will help you estimate the cooking time needed.

COOKING GUIDELINES:

Conventional Recipe:	Cook on LOW:	Cook on HIGH:
30 to 45 minutes	6 to 10 hours	3 to 4 hours
50 minutes to 3 hours	8 to 15 hours	4 to 6 hours

SELECTING MEAT:

Save money by purchasing tougher, more inexpensive cuts of meat, which actually work better for slow cooker recipes. Top-quality cuts,

such as loin chops and filet mignon, tend to fall apart during long cooking times.

CUTTING VEGETABLES:

Since vegetables often take longer to cook than meats, pay careful attention to the recipe's instructions on how to prepare them. Most often, you'll need to cut them into small, thin pieces and place them near the bottom or side of your slow cooker.

SAVORY
BEEF

Easy Family Burritos

Priss Lindsey ◆ *Albuquerque, NM*

Makes 8 servings

1 (2- to 3-pound) beef roast
1 (24-ounce) jar or 2 (16-ounce) jars salsa
Flour tortillas

1. Place roast in slow cooker; top with salsa. Cover and cook on LOW 8 to 10 hours.

2. Remove meat from slow cooker. Shred with 2 forks. Return to slow cooker; cook another 1 to 2 hours.

3. Serve shredded meat wrapped in tortillas.

Priss says: *Garnish your burritos with any combination of the following: shredded cheese, sour cream, salsa, lettuce, tomato, onion, guacamole, etc. I sometimes make a batch of burrito meat and freeze it in family-sized portions. It's quick and easy to reheat in the microwave on busy nights when there is no time to cook.*

Easy Family Burritos

BBQ Beef Sandwiches

Susan Revely ◆ *Ashland, KY*

Makes 10 to 12 servings

1 (2½- to 3-pound) lean boneless chuck roast
¼ cup ketchup
2 tablespoons brown sugar
2 tablespoons red wine vinegar
1 tablespoon Dijon mustard
1 tablespoon Worcestershire sauce
1 clove garlic, crushed
¼ teaspoon salt
¼ teaspoon liquid smoke flavoring
⅛ teaspoon black pepper
10 to 12 French rolls or sandwich buns

1. Place beef in slow cooker. Combine remaining ingredients except rolls in medium bowl; pour over meat. Cover and cook on LOW 8 to 9 hours.

2. Remove beef from slow cooker; shred with 2 forks. Combine beef with 1 cup sauce from slow cooker. Spoon meat and sauce mixture onto warmed, open-face rolls. Top with additional sauce, if desired.

Susan says: *This recipe keeps beautifully in the fridge once cooked. Just reheat in the microwave or on top of the stove.*

BBQ Beef Sandwich

Slow Cooker Pepper Steak

Carol Wright ◆ *Cartersville, GA*

Makes 6 to 8 servings

     2 tablespoons vegetable oil
     3 pounds sirloin steak, cut into strips
     1 heaping tablespoon (5 to 6 cloves) minced garlic
     1 medium onion, chopped
    ½ cup reduced-sodium soy sauce
     2 teaspoons sugar
     1 teaspoon salt
    ½ teaspoon ground ginger
    ½ teaspoon black pepper
     3 green bell peppers, cored, seeded and cut into strips
    ¼ cup cold water
     1 tablespoon cornstarch
       Hot cooked white rice

1. Heat oil in large skillet over medium-low heat. Brown steak on both sides; sprinkle garlic over top.

2. Transfer steak and pan juices to slow cooker. Add onion, soy sauce, sugar, salt, ginger and black pepper. Stir. Cover and cook on LOW 6 to 8 hours or until meat is tender (up to 10 hours).

3. In final hour of cooking, add bell pepper strips. Before serving, mix together water and cornstarch; add to slow cooker. Remove lid; cook on HIGH to thicken sauce. Serve over hot rice.

Slow Cooker Pepper Steak

Round Steak

Deborah Long ◆ Bridgeport, CT

Makes 4 servings

1 (1½-pound) round steak, trimmed of fat and cut into
    4 equal-size pieces
¼ cup all purpose flour
1 teaspoon black pepper
½ teaspoon salt
1 tablespoon vegetable oil
1 can (10¾ ounces) condensed cream of mushroom soup,
    undiluted
¾ cup water
1 envelope (1 ounce) dried onion soup mix
1 can (4 ounces) sliced mushrooms, drained
1 medium onion, quartered
¼ cup milk
    Salt and black pepper
    Ground sage
    Dried thyme leaves
1 bay leaf

1. Place steak in large plastic bag. Close bag and pound with mallet to tenderize. Combine flour, 1 teaspoon black pepper and ½ teaspoon salt in small bowl; add to bag with steak. Shake to coat meat evenly.

2. Heat oil in large nonstick skillet. Remove steak from bag; shake off excess flour. Add steak to oil in skillet; brown on both sides.

3. Add browned steak, pan juices and remaining ingredients to slow cooker. Cover and cook on LOW 5 to 6 hours or until steak is tender. Remove bay leaf before serving.

TIP If you're trying to choose a lean cut of beef, look for "loin" or "round" in the name, such as sirloin, tenderloin or top round. These are the leanest cuts.

Round Steak

Corned Beef and Cabbage

Makes 6 servings

1 head cabbage (1½ pounds), cut into 6 wedges
4 ounces baby carrots
1 corned beef brisket (3 pounds) with seasoning packet*
4 cups water
⅓ cup prepared mustard (optional)
⅓ cup honey (optional)
Chopped fresh parsley, for garnish (optional)

*If seasoning packet is not perforated, poke several small holes with tip of paring knife.

1. Place cabbage in slow cooker; top with carrots.

2. Place seasoning packet on top of carrots. Place corned beef, fat side up, over seasoning packet and carrots. Add water. Cover and cook on LOW 10 hours.

3. Discard seasoning packet. Just before serving, combine mustard and honey in small bowl and use as dipping sauce, if desired. Sprinkle carrots with chopped parsley, if desired

TIP **For more tender and attractive slices, corned beef should be sliced on the diagonal and against the grain.**

Corned Beef and Cabbage

Swiss Steak

Amy Rivera ◆ Arlington, VA

Makes 8 Servings

1 (2-pound) round steak, cut to fit into slow cooker
All-purpose flour
Salt
Black pepper
1 onion, sliced into thick rings
1 clove garlic, minced
1 can (28 ounces) whole tomatoes, undrained
1 can (10¾ ounces) condensed tomato soup, undiluted
3 medium potatoes, unpeeled, diced
1 package (16 ounces) frozen peas and carrots
1 cup sliced celery
Additional vegetables

1. Dredge steak in flour seasoned with salt and pepper. Shake off excess flour.

2. Place onion and garlic in bottom of slow cooker. Add steak and tomatoes. Cover with tomato soup. Add potatoes, peas and carrots, celery and any additional vegetables. Cover and cook on HIGH 4 to 6 hours or until meat and potatoes are tender.

Amy says: *I sometimes add corn or green beans. Very easy and definitely a family favorite!*

Swiss Steak

Easy Beef Sandwiches

Tosha Romanoff ◆ *Union Bridge, MD*

Makes 6 to 8 servings

1 large onion, sliced
1 (3- to 5-pound) rump roast
1 cup water
1 envelope (1 ounce) au jus mix

Place onion slices in bottom of slow cooker; top with roast. Combine water and au jus mix in small bowl; pour over roast. Cover and cook on LOW 7 to 9 hours.

Tosha says: *Before serving, shred the meat in the slow cooker. Serve on French bread with the liquid from the slow cooker. Try topped with provolone cheese for a fantastic sandwich.*

Glazed Corned Beef

Makes 8 to 10 servings

1½ cups water
1 medium onion, sliced
Shredded fresh orange peel
2 whole cloves, plus additional for decoration
3 to 4 pounds corned beef (round or rump cut)
2 tablespoons frozen orange juice concentrate, thawed
3 tablespoons honey
2 teaspoons prepared mustard

1. Mix water, onion, peel and 2 cloves in slow cooker. Add corned beef, fat side up. Cover and cook on LOW 7 to 9 hours or until fork-tender.

2. Remove corned beef; score top. Insert additional cloves to decorate.

3. About 30 minutes before serving, place corned beef in ovenproof pan. Preheat oven to 375°F. Combine juice concentrate, honey and mustard in medium bowl; spoon over corned beef. Bake 20 to 30 minutes, basting occasionally with glaze.

Easy Beef Sandwich

Beef Roll Ups

Mary Schrank ◆ *Racine, WI*

Makes 4 servings

1 (1½-pound) beef round steak, ½ inch thick
4 slices bacon
½ cup diced green bell pepper
¼ cup diced onion
¼ cup diced celery
1 can (10 ounces) beef gravy

1. Cut steak into 4 pieces. Place 1 bacon slice on each piece.

2. Combine bell pepper, onion, and celery in medium bowl. Place about ¼ cup mixture on each piece of meat. Roll up meat; secure with wooden toothpicks.

3. Wipe beef rolls with paper towels. Place beef in slow cooker. Pour gravy evenly over steaks. Cover and cook on LOW 8 to 10 hours. Skim off fat before serving.

Mary says: *Serve with mashed potatoes or over rice.*

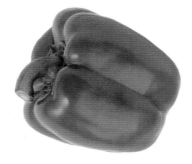

Beef Roll Up

Slow Cooker Stuffed Peppers

Susan Ambrose ◆ *Cabot, PA*

Makes 4 servings

1 pound ground beef
1 package (7 ounces) Spanish rice mix
½ cup diced celery
1 small onion, chopped
1 egg
4 medium green bell peppers, halved lengthwise, cored and seeded
1 can (28 ounces) whole peeled tomatoes, undrained
1 can (10¾ ounces) condensed tomato soup, undiluted
1 cup water

1. Combine beef, rice mix (reserving seasoning packet), celery, onion and egg in large bowl. Divide meat mixture evenly among pepper halves.

2. Pour tomatoes with juice into slow cooker. Arrange filled pepper halves on top of tomatoes. Combine tomato soup, water and rice mix seasoning packet in large bowl. Pour over peppers. Cover and cook on LOW 8 to 10 hours.

Slow Cooker Stuffed Pepper

Smothered Steak

Edye Vanhouten ◆ *Fort Wayne, IN*

Makes 4 servings

1½ to 2 pounds cube steak, cut into 4 pieces
All-purpose flour
1 can (10¾ ounces) condensed cream of mushroom soup, undiluted
1 can (4 ounces) sliced mushrooms
1 envelope (1 ounce) dried onion soup mix

Dust steak lightly with flour. Place in slow cooker. Combine mushroom soup, mushrooms and onion soup mix in medium bowl; pour over steak. Cover and cook on LOW 6 to 8 hours.

Edye says: *Cook all day for dinner tonight!*

Picadillo

Makes 4 servings

1 pound ground beef
1 small onion, chopped
1 clove garlic, minced
1 can (14½ ounces) diced tomatoes, undrained
¼ cup golden raisins
1 tablespoon chili powder
1 tablespoon cider vinegar
½ teaspoon *each*: ground cumin, dried oregano leaves and ground cinnamon
¼ teaspoon red pepper flakes
1 teaspoon salt
¼ cup slivered almonds (optional)

Cook beef, onion and garlic in medium nonstick skillet over medium heat until beef is no longer pink; drain. Place mixture into slow cooker. Add remaining ingredients except salt and almonds to slow cooker. Cover and cook on LOW 6 to 7 hours. Stir in salt. Garnish with almonds, if desired.

Smothered Steak

Peppered Beef Tips

Barbara Messman ◆ *Birmingham, AL*

Makes 2 to 3 servings

**1 pound sirloin beef tips
2 cloves garlic, minced
   Black pepper
1 can (10¾ ounces) condensed French onion soup,
   undiluted
1 can (10¾ ounces) condensed cream of mushroom soup,
   undiluted**

Place beef tips in slow cooker. Sprinkle with garlic and pepper. Pour soups over beef. Cover and cook on LOW 8 to 10 hours.

Barbara says: *Serve over cooked noodles or rice.*

> **TIP** **To peel garlic quickly, place the clove on a cutting board and slightly crush it under the flat side of a chef's knife. Peel away the skin with your fingers.**

Peppered Beef Tips

Easy Homemade Barbecue

Dawn Sunkle ◆ *West Columbia, SC*

Makes 8 to 10 servings

Water
1 (3- to 4-pound) butt roast
Salt
Black pepper
1 bottle (16 ounces) barbecue sauce
Hamburger buns or sandwich rolls

1. Cover bottom of slow cooker with water. Place roast in slow cooker; season with salt and pepper. Cover and cook on LOW 8 to 10 hours.

2. Remove roast from slow cooker; cool 15 minutes. Discard liquid remaining in slow cooker. Using 2 forks, shred cooked roast. Return to slow cooker. Add barbecue sauce; mix well. Cover and cook on HIGH 30 minutes. Spoon onto hamburger buns or rolls.

Dawn says: *Depending on the size of your roast, you may not need to use an entire bottle of barbecue sauce. This recipe is equally tasty when made with pork roast.*

Easy Homemade Barbecue

Slow Cooker Meatloaf

Carolyn Stanley ◆ *Middletown, DE*

Makes 6 servings

- **1½ pounds ground beef**
- **2 eggs, beaten**
- **⅔ cup fine dry bread crumbs**
- **¾ cup milk**
- **2 tablespoons minced onion**
- **1 teaspoon salt**
- **½ teaspoon ground sage**
- **½ cup ketchup**
- **2 tablespoons brown sugar**
- **1 teaspoon dried mustard**

1. Combine beef, eggs, bread crumbs, milk, onion, salt and sage in large bowl. Shape into ball and place in slow cooker. Cover and cook on LOW 5 to 6 hours.

2. Fifteen minutes before serving, combine ketchup, brown sugar and mustard in small bowl. Pour over meatloaf. Cover and cook on HIGH 15 minutes.

Carolyn says: *This is so good I serve it to company!*

Slow Cooker Meatloaf

Smothered Beef Patties

Carol Occhipinti ◆ *Fort Worth, TX*

Makes 8 servings

Worcestershire sauce
Salt
Black pepper
Garlic powder
1 can (14½ ounces) Mexican-style diced tomatoes and
    chilies, undrained, divided
8 frozen beef patties, unthawed
1 onion, cut into 8 slices

Season bottom of slow cooker with small amount of Worcestershire, salt, pepper, garlic powder and 2 tablespoons tomatoes and chilies. Place 1 frozen beef patty on seasonings. Season top of patty with more of same seasonings. Place slice of onion on top of seasonings and patty. Repeat layers. Cover and cook on LOW 8 hours.

Carol says: *Serve with mashed potatoes and Caesar salad. Also delicious with steamed rice.*

Smothered Beef Patty

Spicy Italian Beef

Barbara Mohrle ◆ *Dallas, TX*

Makes 8 to 10 servings

1 (3- to 4-pound) boneless chuck roast
1 jar (12 ounces) pepperoncini (mild salad peppers)
1 can (15 ounces) beef broth
1 can (12 ounces) beer
1 package (1 ounce) Italian salad dressing mix
1 loaf French bread, thickly sliced
10 slices provolone cheese (optional)

1. Trim visible fat from roast. Cut roast, if necessary, to fit into slow cooker, leaving meat in as many large pieces as possible.

2. Drain peppers; pull off stem ends. Add to slow cooker along with broth, beer and dressing mix; do not stir. Cover and cook on LOW 8 to 10 hours.

3. Remove meat from sauce; shred with 2 forks. Return shredded meat to slow cooker; stir.

4. Serve on French bread slice, topped with cheese, if desired. Add sauce and peppers as desired.

Spicy Italian Beef

Autumn Delight

Regina Hill ◆ Burnsville, NC

Makes 4 to 6 servings

> **4 to 6 cube steaks**
> **Olive oil**
> **2 to 3 cans (10¾ ounces each) condensed cream of**
> **   mushroom soup**
> **1 to 1½ cups water**
> **1 envelope (1 ounce) dried onion or mushroom soup mix**

1. Lightly brown cube steaks in oil in large nonstick skillet over medium heat.

2. Place browned cube steaks in slow cooker. Add cans of soup with water as instructed on soup cans (½ cup water per can of soup). Add soup mix; stir to combine. Cover and cook on LOW 4 to 6 hours.

Regina says: *This is a wonderfully easy entrée. Enjoy!*

Autumn Delight

Easy Beefy Sandwiches

Kristen Grotewiel ◆ *St. Charles, MO*

Makes 6 to 8 servings

1 (2- to 4-pound) rump roast
1 envelope (1 ounce) Italian salad dressing mix
1 envelope (1 ounce) dried onion soup mix
2 beef bouillon cubes
2 tablespoons prepared yellow mustard
   Garlic powder
   Onion powder
   Salt
   Black pepper
1 to 1½ cups water

Place roast, salad dressing mix, onion soup mix, bouillon cubes and mustard in slow cooker. Season to taste with garlic powder, onion powder, salt and pepper. Add enough water to cover. Cover and cook on LOW 8 to 10 hours.

Kristen says: *Slice roast and serve with provolone, mozzarella or Lorraine Swiss cheese on hard rolls.*

Easy Beefy Sandwich

Steak San Marino

Makes 4 servings

¼ **cup all-purpose flour**
1 **teaspoon salt**
½ **teaspoon black pepper**
4 **beef round steaks, about 1 inch thick**
1 **can (8 ounces) tomato sauce**
2 **carrots, chopped**
½ **onion, chopped**
1 **rib celery, chopped**
1 **teaspoon dried Italian seasoning**
½ **teaspoon Worcestershire sauce**
1 **bay leaf**
   Hot cooked rice

1. Combine flour, salt and pepper in small bowl. Dredge each steak in flour mixture. Place in slow cooker. Combine tomato sauce, carrots, onion, celery, Italian seasoning, Worcestershire and bay leaf in small bowl; pour into slow cooker. Cover and cook on LOW 8 to 10 hours or on HIGH 4 to 5 hours.

2. Remove and discard bay leaf. Serve steaks and sauce over rice.

Steak San Marino

Beef with Mushroom and Red Wine Gravy

Anne Colville Roberts ◆ Bellville, WI

Makes 6 servings

1½ pounds well-trimmed beef stew meat, cut into 1-inch cubes
2 medium onions, cut into ½-inch wedges
1 (8-ounce) package sliced baby button, cremini or other fresh mushrooms
1 envelope beefy onion soup mix
3 tablespoons cornstarch
⅛ teaspoon salt
⅛ teaspoon black pepper
1½ cups dry red wine

Place beef, onions and mushrooms in slow cooker. Add soup mix over top. Sprinkle with cornstarch, salt and pepper. Pour wine over all. Cover and cook on LOW 10 to 12 hours or on HIGH 5 to 6 hours.

Anne says: *It's like beef bourguignon...without the fat.*

Dad's Dill Beef Roast

Edward Felauer ◆ *Hortonville, WI*

1 (3- to 4-pound) beef roast
1 large jar whole dill pickles, undrained

Place beef in slow cooker. Pour pickles with juice over top of beef. Cover and cook on LOW 8 to 10 hours. Shred beef with two forks.

Edward says: *Pile this beef onto a toasted roll or bun, and you'll have an out-of-this-world sandwich! Or, for an easy dinner variation, serve it with mashed potatoes.*

Beef and Vegetables in Rich Burgundy Sauce

Makes 6 to 8 servings

1 package (8 ounces) sliced mushrooms
1 package (8 ounces) baby carrots
1 medium green bell pepper, cut into thin strips
1 boneless chuck roast (2½ pounds)
1 can (10½ ounces) golden mushroom soup
¼ cup dry red wine or beef broth
1 tablespoon Worcestershire sauce
1 package (1 ounce) dried onion soup mix
¼ teaspoon black pepper
2 tablespoons water
3 tablespoons cornstarch
4 cups hot cooked noodles
Chopped fresh parsley (optional)

1. Place mushrooms, carrots and bell pepper in slow cooker. Place roast on top of vegetables. Combine soup, wine, Worcestershire, soup mix and black pepper in medium bowl; mix well. Pour soup mixture over roast. Cover and cook on LOW 8 to 10 hours.

2. Blend water into cornstarch in cup until smooth; set aside. Transfer roast to cutting board; cover with foil. Let stand 10 to 15 minutes before slicing.

3. Turn slow cooker to HIGH. Stir cornstarch mixture into vegetable mixture; cover and cook 10 minutes or until thickened. Serve over cooked noodles. Garnish with parsley, if desired.

Beef and Vegetables in Rich Burgundy Sauce

Beef and Parsnip Stroganoff

Makes 4 servings

1 beef bouillon cube
¾ cup boiling water
¾ pound well-trimmed boneless top round beef steak,
    1 inch thick
    Nonstick olive oil cooking spray
2 cups cubed peeled parsnips or potatoes*
1 medium onion, halved and thinly sliced
¾ pound mushrooms, sliced
2 teaspoons minced garlic
¼ teaspoon black pepper
¼ cup water
1 tablespoon plus 1½ teaspoons all-purpose flour
3 tablespoons reduced-fat sour cream
1½ teaspoons Dijon mustard
¼ teaspoon cornstarch
1 tablespoon chopped fresh parsley
4 ounces cholesterol-free wide noodles, cooked without
    salt, drained and kept hot

*If using potatoes, cut into 1-inch chunks and do not sauté.

1. Dissolve bouillon cube in ¾ cup boiling water; cool. Meanwhile, cut steak into 2×½-inch strips. Spray large nonstick skillet with cooking spray; heat over high heat. Cook and stir beef about 4 minutes or until meat begins to brown and is barely pink. Transfer beef and juices to slow cooker.

2. Spray same skillet with cooking spray; heat over high heat. Cook and stir parsnips and onion 4 minutes or until browned. Add mushrooms, garlic and pepper; cook and stir 5 minutes or until tender. Mix with beef in slow cooker.

3. Stir ¼ cup water into flour in small bowl until smooth. Stir mixture into cooled bouillon; add to slow cooker. Cover and cook on LOW 4½ to 5 hours or until beef and parsnips are tender.

4. Turn off slow cooker. Remove beef and vegetables to large bowl, reserving cooking liquid. Blend sour cream, mustard and cornstarch in medium bowl. Gradually add reserved liquid to sour cream mixture; stir well. Stir sour cream mixture into beef and vegetables. Sprinkle with parsley; serve over noodles. Garnish, if desired.

Beef and Parsnip Stroganoff

SUCCULENT
PORK

Honey Ribs

Donna Urbanek ◆ Levittown, PA

Makes 4 servings

> 1 can (10¾ ounces) condensed beef consommé, undiluted
> ½ cup water
> 3 tablespoons soy sauce
> 2 tablespoons maple syrup
> 2 tablespoons honey
> 2 tablespoons barbecue sauce
> ½ teaspoon dry mustard
> 2 pounds extra-lean baby back ribs

1. Combine all ingredients except ribs in slow cooker; mix well.

2. Add ribs to slow cooker. (If ribs are especially fatty, broil 10 minutes before adding to slow cooker.) Cover and cook on LOW 6 to 8 hours or on HIGH 3 to 4 hours.

Donna says: *Delicious alone, but even better served over rice.*

TIP Choose fresh pork that is pale pink in color with a small amount of marbling and firm, white (not yellow) fat.

Honey Ribs

Cantonese Pork

Stacy Pineault ◆ *Mahwah, NJ*

Makes 8 servings

1 tablespoon vegetable oil
2 pounds pork tenderloin, cut into strips
1 can (8 ounces) diced pineapple
1 can (8 ounces) tomato sauce
2 cans (4 ounces each) sliced mushrooms, drained
1 medium onion, thinly sliced
3 tablespoons brown sugar
2 tablespoons Worcestershire sauce
1½ teaspoons salt
1½ teaspoons white vinegar
    Hot cooked rice

1. Heat oil in large nonstick skillet over medium-low heat. Brown pork on both sides. Drain excess fat.

2. Place all ingredients in slow cooker. Cook on HIGH 4 hours or on LOW 6 to 8 hours. Serve over rice.

Cantonese Pork

Italian Combo Subs

Valorie Rowland ◆ *Hardin, KY*

Makes 6 servings

1 tablespoon vegetable oil
1 pound round steak, sliced into thin strips
1 pound bulk Italian sausage
1 medium onion, thinly sliced
1 can (4 ounces) sliced mushrooms (optional)
1 green bell pepper, cored, seeded and cut into strips
　　Salt
　　Black pepper
1 jar (25 ounces) spaghetti sauce
2 loaves Italian bread, cut into 1-inch-thick slices

1. Heat oil in large skillet over medium-high heat. Gently brown round steak. Remove steak strips to slow cooker. Drain excess fat from skillet.

2. In same skillet, brown Italian sausage until no longer pink. Drain excess fat. Add sausage to slow cooker.

3. Place onion, mushrooms and bell pepper over meat. Add salt and black pepper to taste; cover with spaghetti sauce. Cover and cook on LOW 4 to 6 hours. Serve as a sandwich or over bread slices.

Serving Suggestion: Top with freshly grated Parmesan cheese.

Italian Combo Sub

Simply Delicious Pork

Carol Morris ◆ *Auburn, IN*

Makes 6 servings

1½ pounds boneless pork loin, sliced
4 medium Yellow Delicious apples, cored and sliced
3 tablespoons brown sugar
1 teaspoon cinnamon
½ teaspoon salt

Place pork slices in bottom of slow cooker. Cover with apples. Combine brown sugar, cinnamon and salt in small bowl; sprinkle over apples. Cover and cook on LOW 6 to 8 hours.

Orange Teriyaki Pork

Makes 4 servings

Nonstick cooking spray
1 pound lean pork stew meat, cut into 1-inch cubes
1 package (16 ounces) frozen pepper blend for stir-fry
4 ounces sliced water chestnuts
½ cup orange juice
2 tablespoons quick-cooking tapioca
2 tablespoons packed light brown sugar
2 tablespoons teriyaki sauce
½ teaspoon ground ginger
½ teaspoon dry mustard
1⅓ cups hot cooked rice

1. Spray large nonstick skillet with cooking spray; heat over medium heat until hot. Add pork; brown on all sides. Remove from heat; set aside.

2. Place peppers and water chestnuts in slow cooker. Top with browned pork. Combine orange juice, tapioca, brown sugar, teriyaki sauce, ginger and mustard in large bowl. Pour over pork mixture in slow cooker. Cover and cook on LOW 3 to 4 hours; stir. Serve over rice.

Simply Delicious Pork

Spareribs Simmered in Orange Sauce

Makes 4 to 6 servings

4 pounds country-style pork spareribs
2 tablespoons vegetable oil
2 medium white onions, cut into ¼-inch slices
1 to 2 tablespoons dried ancho chilies, seeded and finely chopped
½ teaspoon ground cinnamon
¼ teaspoon ground cloves
1 can (16 ounces) tomatoes, undrained
2 cloves garlic
½ cup orange juice
⅓ cup packed brown sugar
⅓ cup dry white wine
1 teaspoon shredded orange peel
½ teaspoon salt
1 to 2 tablespoons cider vinegar
Orange wedges (optional)

1. Trim excess fat from ribs. Cut into individual riblets. Heat oil in large skillet over medium heat. Add ribs; cook 10 minutes or until browned on all sides. Remove to plate. Remove and discard all but 2 tablespoons drippings from skillet. Add onions, chilies, cinnamon and cloves. Cook and stir 4 minutes or until softened. Transfer onion mixture to slow cooker.

2. Process tomatoes and garlic in food processor or blender until smooth.

3. Combine tomato mixture, orange juice, sugar, wine, orange peel and salt in slow cooker. Add ribs; stir to coat. Cover and cook on LOW 5 hours or until ribs are fork-tender. Remove ribs. Ladle liquid into medium bowl; let stand 5 minutes. Skim and discard fat. Stir in vinegar. Serve sauce over ribs. Serve with carrots and garnish with orange wedges, if desired.

Spareribs Simmered in Orange Sauce

Cheesy Pork and Potatoes

Makes 6 servings

½ **pound ground pork, cooked and crumbled**
½ **cup finely crushed saltine crackers**
⅓ **cup barbecue sauce**
1 **egg**
3 **tablespoons margarine**
1 **tablespoon vegetable oil**
4 **potatoes, peeled and thinly sliced**
1 **medium onion, thinly sliced**
1 **cup grated mozzarella cheese**
⅔ **cup evaporated milk**
1 **teaspoon salt**
¼ **teaspoon paprika**
⅛ **teaspoon black pepper**
   Chopped fresh parsley

1. Combine pork, crackers, barbecue sauce and egg in large bowl; shape mixture into 6 patties.

2. Heat margarine and oil in medium skillet. Sauté potatoes and onion until lightly browned. Drain and place in slow cooker.

3. Combine cheese, milk, salt, paprika and pepper in medium bowl. Pour into slow cooker. Layer pork patties on top. Cover and cook on LOW 3 to 5 hours. Garnish with parsley.

Cheesy Pork and Potatoes

Feijoada Completa

Makes 10 to 12 servings

**1½ pounds country-style pork ribs or pork spareribs
1 corned beef brisket (1½ pounds)
½ pound smoked link sausage, such as Polish or andouille
½ pound fresh link sausage, such as bratwurst or breakfast
    links
3 cups water
1 can (15½ ounces) black beans, rinsed and drained
1 cup chopped onion
4 cloves garlic, minced
1 jalapeño pepper,* seeded and chopped
Chili-Lemon Sauce (recipe follows)**

*Jalapeño peppers can sting and irritate the skin; wear rubber gloves when handling
peppers and do not touch eyes. Wash hands after handling.*

1. Trim excess fat from ribs; discard. Combine all ingredients except Chili-Lemon Sauce in slow cooker; stir to mix well. Cover and cook on LOW 7 to 8 hours or until meats are fork-tender. Meanwhile, prepare Chili-Lemon Sauce.

2. Remove meats to cutting board. Slice corned beef; place on large serving platter. Arrange remaining meat around corned beef. Cover meat and keep warm.

3. Drain liquid from beans, leaving just enough liquid so beans are moist. Transfer to serving bowl. Serve with Chili-Lemon Sauce. Garnish as desired.

Chili-Lemon Sauce

**¾ cup lemon juice
1 small onion, coarsely chopped
3 jalapeño peppers,* seeded and chopped
3 cloves garlic, cut into halves**

*Jalapeño peppers can sting and irritate the skin; wear rubber gloves when handling
peppers and do not touch eyes. Wash hands after handling.*

Place all ingredients in food processor or blender; process until smooth. Serve at room temperature.

Feijoada Completa

Mediterranean Meatball Ratatouille

Makes 6 (1⅔-cup) servings

2 tablespoons olive oil, divided
1 pound mild Italian sausage, casings removed
1 package (8 ounces) sliced mushrooms
1 small eggplant, diced
1 zucchini, diced
½ cup chopped onion
1 clove garlic, minced
1 teaspoon dried oregano leaves
1 teaspoon salt
½ teaspoon black pepper
1 tablespoon tomato paste
2 tomatoes, diced
2 tablespoons chopped fresh basil
1 teaspoon fresh lemon juice

1. Pour 1 tablespoon olive oil into 5-quart slow cooker. Shape sausage into 1-inch balls. Place half the meatballs in slow cooker. Add half the mushrooms, eggplant and zucchini. Add onion, garlic, ½ teaspoon oregano, ½ teaspoon salt and ¼ teaspoon pepper.

2. Add remaining meatballs, mushrooms, eggplant and zucchini. Add remaining ½ teaspoon oregano, ½ teaspoon salt and ¼ teaspoon pepper. Top with remaining 1 tablespoon olive oil. Cover and cook on LOW 6 to 7 hours.

3. Stir in tomato paste and diced tomatoes. Cover and cook on LOW 15 minutes. Stir in basil and lemon juice; serve. Garnish as desired.

Mediterranean Meatball Ratatouille

Barbara's Pork Chop Dinner

Makes 6 servings

1 tablespoon butter
1 tablespoon olive oil
6 bone-in pork loin chops
1 can (10¾ ounces) condensed cream of chicken soup,
    undiluted
1 can (4 ounces) mushrooms, drained and chopped
¼ cup Dijon mustard
¼ cup chicken broth
2 cloves garlic, minced
½ teaspoon salt
½ teaspoon dried basil leaves
¼ teaspoon black pepper
6 red potatoes, unpeeled, cut into thin slices
1 medium onion, sliced
Chopped fresh parsley

1. Heat butter and oil in large skillet. Brown pork chops on both sides. Set aside.

2. Combine soup, mushrooms, mustard, chicken broth, garlic, salt, basil and pepper in slow cooker. Add potatoes and onion, stirring to coat. Place pork chops on top of potato mixture. Cover and cook on LOW 8 to 10 hours or on HIGH 4 to 5 hours. Sprinkle with parsley.

TIP **To ensure thorough cooking, cut denser vegetables, such as potatoes and carrots, no thicker than one inch before adding to your slow cooker.**

Barbara's Pork Chop Dinner

Shredded Pork Wraps

Makes 6 servings

1 cup salsa, divided
2 tablespoons cornstarch
1 bone-in pork sirloin roast (2 pounds)
6 (8-inch) flour tortillas
⅓ cup shredded reduced-fat Cheddar cheese
3 cups broccoli slaw mix

1. Combine ¼ cup salsa and cornstarch in small bowl; stir until smooth. Pour mixture into slow cooker. Top with pork roast. Pour remaining ¾ cup salsa over roast. Cover and cook on LOW 6 to 8 hours or until internal temperature reaches 165°F when tested with meat thermometer inserted into thickest part of roast, not touching bone.

2. Remove roast from slow cooker; transfer to cutting board. Cover with foil and let stand 10 to 15 minutes or until cool enough to handle before shredding. Internal temperature will rise 5° to 10°F during stand time. Trim and discard outer fat from pork. Using 2 forks, pull pork into coarse shreds.

3. Divide shredded meat evenly onto each tortilla. Spoon about 2 tablespoons salsa mixture on top of meat in each tortilla. Top evenly with cheese and broccoli slaw mix. Fold bottom edge of tortilla over filling; fold in sides. Roll up completely to enclose filling. Repeat with remaining tortillas. Serve remaining salsa mixture as dipping sauce.

Shredded Pork Wrap

Sweet and Sour Spareribs

Makes 4 servings

4 pounds pork spareribs
2 cups dry sherry or chicken broth
½ cup pineapple, mango or guava juice
⅓ cup chicken broth
2 tablespoons packed light brown sugar
2 tablespoons cider vinegar
2 tablespoons soy sauce
1 clove garlic, minced
½ teaspoon salt
¼ teaspoon black pepper
⅛ teaspoon red pepper flakes
1 tablespoon cornstarch

1. Preheat oven to 400°F. Place ribs in foil-lined shallow roasting pan. Bake 30 minutes, turning ribs after 15 minutes. Remove from oven. Slice meat into 2-rib portions. Place ribs in 5-quart slow cooker. Add remaining ingredients except cornstarch to slow cooker. Cover and cook on LOW 6 hours. Uncover and skim fat from liquid.

2. Combine cornstarch and ¼ cup liquid from slow cooker in small bowl; stir until smooth. Pour mixture back into slow cooker; mix well. Cover and cook on HIGH 10 minutes or until slightly thickened.

Sweet and Sour Spareribs

PIPIN' HOT
POULTRY

Oriental Chicken Wings

Makes 32 appetizer servings

32 pieces chicken wing drums and flats
1 cup chopped red onion
1 cup soy sauce
¾ cup light brown sugar
¼ cup dry cooking sherry
2 tablespoons chopped fresh ginger
2 cloves garlic, minced
Chopped chives

1. Broil chicken wings, about 5 minutes per side. Transfer chicken to slow cooker.

2. Stir together onion, soy sauce, brown sugar, sherry, ginger and garlic in large bowl. Add to slow cooker; stir to combine. Cover and cook on LOW 5 to 6 hours or on HIGH 2 to 3 hours. Sprinkle with chives.

> **TIP** **Serve these wings with noodles or rice and vegetables for a great main-dish offering!**

Oriental Chicken Wings

Chinese Cashew Chicken

Barb Gartzke ◆ *Sullivan, WI*

Makes 4 servings

- **1 pound bean sprouts (fresh or canned)**
- **2 cups sliced cooked chicken**
- **1 can (10¾ ounces) condensed cream of mushroom soup, undiluted**
- **1 cup sliced celery**
- **½ cup chopped green onion**
- **1 can (4 ounces) mushroom pieces, drained**
- **3 tablespoons butter**
- **1 tablespoon soy sauce**
- **1 cup cashews**

Combine all ingredients except cashews in slow cooker. Cover and cook on LOW 4 to 6 hours or on HIGH 3 to 4 hours. Just before serving, stir in cashews.

Barb says: *Serve with rice or noodles.*

Chicken Teriyaki

Makes 4 servings

- **1 pound boneless skinless chicken tenders**
- **1 can (6 ounces) pineapple juice**
- **¼ cup soy sauce**
- **1 tablespoon sugar**
- **1 tablespoon minced fresh ginger**
- **1 tablespoon minced garlic**
- **1 tablespoon vegetable oil**
- **1 tablespoon molasses**
- **24 cherry tomatoes (optional)**
- **2 cups hot cooked rice**

Combine all ingredients except rice in slow cooker. Cover and cook on LOW 2 hours. Serve chicken and sauce over rice.

Chinese Cashew Chicken

Cheesy Slow Cooker Chicken

Joan VandenNoven ◆ *Beloit, WI*

Makes 6 servings

6 boneless skinless chicken breast halves
Salt
Black pepper
Garlic powder
2 cans (10¾ ounces each) condensed cream of
    chicken soup, undiluted
1 can (10¾ ounces) condensed Cheddar cheese soup,
    undiluted
Chopped fresh parsley (optional)

1. Place 3 chicken breast halves in slow cooker. Sprinkle with salt, pepper and garlic powder. Repeat with remaining three breasts.

2. Mix soups together in medium bowl; pour over chicken. Cover and cook on LOW 6 to 8 hours. Garnish with chopped fresh parsley before serving, if desired.

Joan says: *The sauce is wonderful over noodles, rice or mashed potatoes.*

Cheesy Slow Cooker Chicken

Meatball Grinders

Makes 4 servings

1 can (15 ounces) diced tomatoes, drained and juices reserved
1 can (8 ounces) reduced-sodium tomato sauce
¼ cup chopped onion
2 tablespoons tomato paste
1 teaspoon dried Italian seasoning
1 pound ground chicken
½ cup fresh whole wheat or white bread crumbs (1 slice bread)
1 egg white, lightly beaten
3 tablespoons finely chopped fresh parsley
2 cloves garlic, minced
¼ teaspoon salt
⅛ teaspoon black pepper
  Nonstick cooking spray
4 small hard rolls, split
2 tablespoons fresh grated Parmesan cheese

1. Combine diced tomatoes, ½ cup reserved juice, tomato sauce, onion, tomato paste and Italian seasoning in slow cooker. Cover and cook on LOW 3 to 4 hours or until onion is soft.

2. During last 30 minutes of cooking, prepare meatballs. Combine chicken, bread crumbs, egg white, parsley, garlic, salt and pepper in large bowl. With wet hands, form mixture into 12 to 16 meatballs. Spray medium nonstick skillet with cooking spray; heat over medium heat until hot. Add meatballs; cook about 8 to 10 minutes or until well-browned on all sides.

3. Remove meatballs to slow cooker; cook 1 to 2 hours or until meatballs are no longer pink in center and are heated through. Place 3 to 4 meatballs in each roll. Spoon sauce evenly over meatballs. Sprinkle with cheese.

Meatball Grinder

Chicken and Stuffing

Anna Ertl ◆ Franksville, WI

Makes 4 to 6 servings

½ **cup flour**
¾ **teaspoon seasoned salt**
   Black pepper
4 to 6 boneless skinless chicken breast halves
¼ **cup butter**
**2 cans (10¾ ounces each) condensed cream of mushroom
   soup, undiluted**
½ **cup water**
1 package (12 ounces) seasoned stuffing mix

1. Combine flour, seasoned salt and pepper in large resealable food storage bag. Dredge chicken in flour mixture. Melt butter in large skillet over medium-low heat. Brown both sides of chicken in butter. Place chicken in slow cooker.

2. Mix together soup and water in medium bowl; pour soup mixture over top of chicken. Follow package directions for stuffing, decreasing liquid by half. Add to slow cooker over chicken. Cover and cook on HIGH 3 to 4 hours.

Herbed Turkey Breast with Orange Sauce

Makes 4 to 6 servings

1 large onion, chopped
3 cloves garlic, minced
1 teaspoon dried rosemary leaves
½ **teaspoon black pepper**
2 to 3 pounds boneless skinless turkey breast
1½ **cups orange juice**

1. Place onion in slow cooker. Combine garlic, rosemary and pepper in small bowl; set aside. Make slices in turkey, about ¾ of the way through breast, at 2-inch intervals. Stuff slices with garlic mixture.

2. Place turkey in slow cooker. Pour orange juice over turkey. Cover and cook on LOW 7 to 8 hours or until turkey is no longer pink in center.

Chicken and Stuffing

Heidi's Chicken Supreme

Kim Adams ◆ *Manchester, MO*

Makes 6 servings

**1 can (10¾ ounces) condensed cream of chicken soup,
    undiluted**
1 envelope (1 ounce) dried onion soup mix
6 boneless skinless chicken breast halves
**½ cup canned bacon crumbles *or* ½ pound bacon, fried and
    crumbled**
1 carton (16 ounces) reduced-fat sour cream

Spray slow cooker cooking surface with nonstick cooking spray. Mix soup with
soup mix in medium bowl. Layer chicken breasts and soup mixture in slow
cooker. Sprinkle bacon crumbles over top. Cover and cook on HIGH 4 hours
or on LOW 8 hours. During last hour of cooking, add sour cream; stir.

Kim says: *This is delicious over noodles. You can also use condensed
cream of mushroom or celery soup, if that is what you have on hand.*

Heidi's Chicken Supreme

Spicy Shredded Chicken

Amanda Neelley ◆ *Spring Hill, TN*

Makes 6 servings

6 boneless skinless chicken breast halves
1 jar of your favorite prepared salsa

Place chicken in slow cooker. Cover with salsa. Cover and cook on LOW 6 to 8 hours. Shred chicken with two forks before serving.

Amanda says: *Serve on warm flour tortillas with taco fixings.*

Mile-High Enchilada Pie

Makes 4 to 6 servings

8 (6-inch) corn tortillas
1 jar (12 ounces) prepared salsa
1 can (15½ ounces) kidney beans, rinsed and drained
1 cup shredded cooked chicken
1 cup shredded Monterey Jack cheese with jalapeño peppers

Prepare foil handles for slow cooker (see below); place in slow cooker. Place 1 tortilla on bottom of slow cooker. Top with small amount of salsa, beans, chicken and cheese. Continue layering, using remaining ingredients and ending with cheese. Cover and cook on LOW 6 to 8 hours or on HIGH 3 to 4 hours. Pull out by foil handles.

Foil Handles: Tear off three 18×2-inch strips of heavy foil, or use regular foil folded to double thickness. Crisscross foil strips in spoke design.

Spicy Shredded Chicken

French Country Slow Cooker Chicken

Teri Lindquist ◆ *Gurnee, IL*

Makes 6 to 8 servings

1 medium onion, chopped
4 carrots, sliced
4 ribs celery, sliced
1 can (4 ounces) sliced mushrooms, drained
6 to 8 boneless skinless chicken breast halves, cut up
1 teaspoon dried thyme leaves
½ teaspoon dried tarragon leaves
  Salt
  Black pepper
1 can (10¾ ounces) condensed cream of chicken soup, undiluted
1 envelope (1 ounce) dried onion soup mix
⅓ cup white wine or apple juice
2 tablespoons cornstarch

1. Place onion, carrots, celery and mushrooms in bottom of slow cooker. Arrange chicken pieces over vegetables. Sprinkle chicken with thyme, tarragon, salt and pepper. Pour soup over chicken and seasonings. Sprinkle onion soup mix over chicken and soup. Cover and cook on HIGH 3 to 4 hours, stirring once.

2. Twenty minutes before serving, whisk together wine and cornstarch in small bowl; stir until smooth. Pour mixture over chicken; mix well. Uncover and cook on HIGH 15 minutes or until sauce thickens. Stir again before serving.

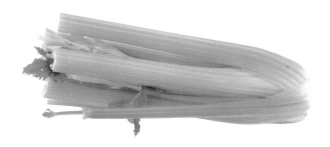

French Country Slow Cooker Chicken

Chili Turkey Loaf

Makes 8 servings

  2 pounds ground turkey
  1 cup chopped onion
  ⅔ cup Italian-style seasoned dry bread crumbs
  ½ cup chopped green bell pepper
  ½ cup chili sauce
  4 cloves garlic, minced
  2 eggs, slightly beaten
  2 tablespoons horseradish mustard
  1 teaspoon salt
  ½ teaspoon dried Italian seasoning
  ¼ teaspoon black pepper
     Prepared salsa (optional)

1. Make foil handles for slow cooker (see page 82). Combine all ingredients except salsa in large bowl. Shape into round loaf and place on top of foil strips. Transfer to bottom of slow cooker, using foil handles. Cover and cook on LOW 4½ to 5 hours or until juices run clear and internal temperature reaches 170°F.

2. Remove loaf from slow cooker, using foil handles. Place on serving plate. Let stand 5 minutes before serving. Slice and top with salsa, if desired.

Chili Turkey Loaf

Creamy Chicken and Mushrooms

Lisa Langston ◆ *Conroe, TX*

Makes 3 to 4 servings

  1 teaspoon salt
  ½ teaspoon black pepper
  ¼ teaspoon paprika
  3 boneless skinless chicken breast halves, cut up
1¾ teaspoons chicken bouillon granules
1½ cups sliced fresh mushrooms, drained
  ½ cup sliced green onions
  1 cup white wine
  ½ cup water
  1 can (5 ounces) evaporated milk
  5 teaspoons cornstarch
     Hot cooked rice

1. Combine salt, pepper and paprika in small bowl; sprinkle over chicken. Rub spices into chicken.

2. Alternate layers of chicken, bouillon, mushrooms and green onions in slow cooker. Pour wine and water over top. Cover; cook on HIGH 3 hours or on LOW 5 to 6 hours. Remove chicken and vegetables to platter; cover to keep warm.

3. Combine evaporated milk and cornstarch in small saucepan until smooth. Gradually stir in 2 cups liquid from slow cooker. Bring to a boil. Boil 1 minute or until thickened, stirring constantly. To serve, spoon sauce over chicken and rice.

Creamy Chicken and Mushrooms

Forty-Clove Chicken

Makes 4 to 6 servings

1 frying chicken (3 pounds), cut into serving pieces
Salt
Black pepper
1 to 2 tablespoons olive oil
¼ cup dry white wine
⅛ cup dry vermouth
2 tablespoons chopped fresh parsley *or* 2 teaspoons dried
   parsley leaves
2 teaspoons dried basil leaves
1 teaspoon dried oregano leaves
Pinch of red pepper flakes
40 cloves garlic (about 2 large heads*), peeled
4 ribs celery, sliced
Juice and peel of 1 lemon
Fresh herbs (optional)

*The whole garlic bulb is called a head.

1. Remove skin from chicken, if desired. Sprinkle chicken with salt and pepper. Heat oil in large skillet over medium heat. Add chicken; cook 10 minutes or until browned on all sides. Remove to platter.

2. Combine wine, vermouth, parsley, basil, oregano and red pepper flakes in large bowl. Add garlic and celery; coat well. Transfer garlic and celery to slow cooker with slotted spoon.

3. Add chicken to remaining herb mixture; coat well. Place chicken on top of celery in slow cooker. Sprinkle lemon juice and peel into slow cooker; add remaining herb mixture. Cover and cook on LOW 6 hours or until chicken is no longer pink in center. Garnish with fresh herbs, if desired.

Forty-Clove Chicken

Hot & Sour Chicken

Lynda McCormick ◆ *Burkburnett, TX*

Makes 4 to 6 servings

4 to 6 boneless skinless chicken breast halves
1 envelope (1 ounce) dried hot-and-sour soup mix
1 cup chicken or vegetable broth

Place chicken in slow cooker. Add soup mix. Pour broth over top. Cover and cook on LOW 5 to 6 hours. Garnish as desired.

Lynda says: *This dish can be served over steamed white rice and topped with crispy Chinese noodles. Or, for a colorful variation, serve it over a bed of snow peas and sugar snap peas tossed with diced red bell pepper.*

Sweet Jalapeño Mustard Turkey Thighs

Makes 6 servings

3 turkey thighs, skin removed
¾ cup honey mustard
½ cup orange juice
1 tablespoon cider vinegar
1 to 2 fresh jalapeño peppers,* finely chopped
1 teaspoon Worcestershire sauce
1 clove garlic, minced
½ teaspoon grated orange peel

*Jalapeño peppers can sting and irritate the skin; wear rubber gloves when handling peppers and do not touch eyes. Wash hands after handling.

Place turkey thighs in single layer in slow cooker. Combine remaining ingredients in large bowl. Pour mixture over turkey thighs. Cover and cook on LOW 5 to 6 hours.

Hot & Sour Chicken

Chicken Parisienne

Maureen Baisden ◆ *Columbus, OH*

Makes 6 servings

6 boneless skinless chicken breast halves, cubed
Salt
Black pepper
½ teaspoon paprika
1 can (10¾ ounces) condensed cream of mushroom or
    cream of chicken soup, undiluted
2 cans (4 ounces each) sliced mushrooms, drained
½ cup dry white wine
1 cup sour cream
6 cups hot cooked egg noodles

1. Place chicken cubes in slow cooker. Sprinkle with salt, pepper and paprika.

2. Pour soup, mushrooms and wine over chicken; mix well. Cover and cook on HIGH 2 to 3 hours. In last 30 minutes of cooking, add sour cream. Serve over noodles. Garnish as desired.

Maureen says: *For a taste-pleasing variation, try this dish over rice instead of noodles.*

Chicken Parisienne

Mu Shu Turkey

Makes 6 servings

1 can (16 ounces) plums, rinsed, drained, and pitted
½ cup orange juice
¼ cup finely chopped onion
1 tablespoon minced fresh ginger
¼ teaspoon ground cinnamon
**1 pound boneless skinless turkey breast, cut into thin
    strips**
6 (7-inch) flour tortillas
3 cups coleslaw mix

1. Place plums in blender or food processor. Cover and blend until almost smooth. Combine plums, orange juice, onion, ginger and cinnamon in slow cooker; mix well. Place turkey strips over plum mixture. Cover and cook on LOW 3 to 4 hours.

2. Remove turkey strips from slow cooker and divide evenly among tortillas. Spoon about 2 tablespoons plum sauce over turkey. Top evenly with coleslaw mix. Fold bottom edge of tortilla over filling; fold in sides. Roll up to completely enclose filling. Repeat with remaining tortillas. Use remaining plum sauce for dipping.

TIP **To mince ginger quickly, cut and peel a small chunk and put it through a garlic press.**

Mu Shu Turkey

Sweet Chicken Curry

Makes 4 servings

1 pound boneless skinless chicken breasts, cut into 1-inch pieces
1 large green or red bell pepper, cut into 1-inch pieces
1 large onion, sliced
1 large tomato, seeded and chopped
½ cup prepared mango chutney
¼ cup water
2 tablespoons cornstarch
1½ teaspoons curry powder
1⅓ cups hot cooked rice

1. Place chicken, bell pepper and onion in slow cooker. Top with tomato.

2. Combine chutney, water, cornstarch and curry powder in large bowl. Pour chutney mixture over chicken mixture in slow cooker. Cover and cook on LOW 3½ to 4½ hours. Serve over rice.

Sweet Chicken Curry

Continental Chicken

Helen Syfie ◆ *Omaha, NE*

Makes 4 servings

- **1 package (2¼ ounces) dried beef, cut up**
- **4 boneless skinless chicken breast halves**
- **4 slices lean bacon**
- **1 can (10¾ ounces) condensed cream of mushroom soup, undiluted**
- **¼ cup all-purpose flour**
- **¼ cup low-fat sour cream**

1. Spray slow cooker cooking surface with nonstick cooking spray. Place dried beef in bottom of slow cooker. Wrap each piece of chicken with one bacon strip. Place wrapped chicken on top of dried beef.

2. Combine soup, flour and sour cream in medium bowl until smooth. Pour over chicken. Cover and cook on LOW 7 to 9 hours or on HIGH 3 to 4 hours.

Helen says: *Serve over hot buttered noodles.*

Lemony Roasted Chicken

Makes 6 servings

- **1 fryer or roasting chicken (3 to 4 pounds)**
- **½ cup chopped onion**
- **2 tablespoons butter**
- **Juice of one lemon**
- **1 tablespoon fresh parsley**
- **2 teaspoons grated lemon peel**
- **¼ teaspoon salt**
- **¼ teaspoon dried thyme leaves**

Rinse chicken and pat dry with paper towels. Remove and discard any excess fat. Place onion in chicken cavity and rub skin with butter. Place chicken in slow cooker. Squeeze lemon juice over chicken. Sprinkle with parsley, grated lemon peel, salt and thyme. Cover and cook on LOW 6 to 8 hours.

Continental Chicken

Coq au Vin

Makes 6 servings

4 slices thick-cut bacon
2 cups frozen pearl onions, thawed
1 cup sliced button mushrooms
1 clove garlic, minced
1 teaspoon dried thyme leaves
⅛ teaspoon black pepper
6 boneless skinless chicken breast halves (about 2 pounds)
½ cup dry red wine
¾ cup reduced-sodium chicken broth
¼ cup tomato paste
3 tablespoons all-purpose flour
Hot cooked egg noodles (optional)

1. Cook bacon in medium skillet over medium heat. Drain and crumble.

2. Layer ingredients in slow cooker in the following order: onions, bacon, mushrooms, garlic, thyme, pepper, chicken, wine and broth. Cover and cook on LOW 6 to 8 hours.

3. Remove chicken and vegetables; cover and keep warm. Ladle ½ cup cooking liquid into small bowl; allow to cool slightly. Turn slow cooker to HIGH; cover.

4. Combine reserved liquid, tomato paste and flour in medium bowl until smooth. Return mixture to slow cooker; cover and cook 15 minutes or until thickened. Serve chicken and vegetables with sauce over hot noodles, if desired.

Coq au Vin

Hearty Calico Bean Dip

Heather Daoust ◆ *Ashland, WI*

Makes 12 servings

- ¾ **pound ground beef, cooked and drained**
- ½ **pound sliced bacon, cooked, drained and crumbled**
- 1 **can (16 ounces) baked beans**
- 1 **can (15½ ounces) Great Northern beans, rinsed and drained**
- 1 **can (15 ounces) kidney beans, rinsed and drained**
- 1 **small onion, chopped**
- ½ **cup brown sugar**
- ½ **cup ketchup**
- 1 **tablespoon vinegar**
- 1 **teaspoon prepared mustard**

Combine all ingredients in large bowl; place in slow cooker. Cover and cook on LOW 4 hours or on HIGH 2 hours. Garnish as desired.

Heather says: *Place in serving dish and scoop up beans with tortilla chips.*

Hearty Calico Bean Dip

Mediterranean Red Potatoes

Makes 4 servings

2 medium red potatoes, cut in half lengthwise, then crosswise into pieces
⅔ cup fresh or frozen pearl onions
Nonstick garlic-flavored cooking spray
¾ teaspoon dried Italian seasoning
¼ teaspoon black pepper
1 small tomato, seeded and chopped
2 ounces feta cheese, crumbled
2 tablespoons chopped black olives

1. Place potatoes and onions in 1½-quart soufflé dish. Spray potatoes and onions with cooking spray; toss to coat. Add Italian seasoning and pepper; mix well. Cover dish tightly with foil.

2. Tear off 3 (18×3-inch) strips of heavy-duty aluminum foil. Cross strips so they resemble wheel spokes. Place soufflé dish in center of strips. Pull foil strips up and over dish and place dish in slow cooker.

3. Pour hot water to about 1½ inches from top of soufflé dish. Cover and cook on LOW 7 to 8 hours.

4. Use foil handles to lift dish from slow cooker. Stir tomato, feta cheese and olives into potato mixture.

Mediterranean Red Potatoes

Escalloped Corn

Makes 6 servings

2 tablespoons butter or margarine
½ cup chopped onion
3 tablespoons all-purpose flour
1 cup milk
4 cups frozen corn, thawed and divided
½ teaspoon salt
½ teaspoon dried thyme leaves
¼ teaspoon black pepper
⅛ teaspoon ground nutmeg
   Fresh thyme (optional)

1. Heat butter in small saucepan over medium heat. Add onion; cook and stir 5 minutes or until tender. Add flour. Cook over medium heat 1 minute, stirring constantly. Stir in milk and heat to a boil. Boil 1 minute or until thickened, stirring constantly.

2. Process half the corn in food processor or blender until coarsely chopped.

3. Combine milk mixture, processed and whole corn, salt, dried thyme, pepper and nutmeg in slow cooker. Cover and cook on LOW 3½ to 4 hours or until mixture is bubbly around edge. Garnish with fresh thyme, if desired.

Variation: If desired, add ½ cup (2 ounces) shredded Cheddar cheese and 2 tablespoons grated Parmesan cheese before serving; stir until melted. Garnish with additional shredded Cheddar cheese, if desired.

Escalloped Corn

Cran-Orange Acorn Squash

Makes 6 servings

3 small carnival or acorn squash
5 tablespoons instant brown rice
3 tablespoons dried cranberries
3 tablespoons diced celery
3 tablespoons minced onion
  Pinch ground or dried sage
1 teaspoon butter, divided
3 tablespoons orange juice
½ cup water

1. Slice off points on bottoms of squash so the squash will stand in slow cooker. Slice off tops; discard. Scoop out seeds; discard. Set squash aside.

2. Combine rice, cranberries, celery, onion and sage in small bowl. Stuff squash with rice mixture; dot with butter. Pour 1 tablespoon orange juice over stuffing in each squash.

3. Stand squash in slow cooker. Pour water into bottom of slow cooker. Cover; cook on LOW about 2½ hours.

Honey Whole-Grain Bread

Makes 10 servings (about 8 slices)

2 cups warm (not hot) whole milk
¼ cup honey
2 tablespoons canola oil
¾ teaspoon salt
1 package active dry yeast
3 cups whole-wheat bread flour, divided
¾ to 1 cup all-purpose unbleached flour, divided

1. Spray 1-quart casserole, soufflé dish or other high-sided baking pan with nonstick cooking spray. Combine milk, honey, oil, salt, yeast, 1½ cups wheat flour and ½ cup all-purpose flour in large bowl of electric mixer. Mix at medium-low speed 2 minutes.

2. Add remaining 1½ cups cups wheat flour and ¼ cup to ½ cup all-purpose flour. If mixer has difficulty mixing dough, mix in remaining flours with wooden spoon.

3. Transfer to prepared pan. Place pan in slow cooker. Cover and cook on HIGH about 3 hours or until edges are browned.

4. Remove from slow cooker. Let stand 5 minutes. Unmold on wire rack to cool.

Classic Cabbage Rolls

Makes 6 servings

   6 cups water
12 large cabbage leaves
   1 pound lean ground lamb
½ cup cooked rice
   1 teaspoon salt
¼ teaspoon dried oregano leaves
¼ teaspoon ground nutmeg
¼ teaspoon black pepper
1½ cups tomato sauce

1. Bring water to a boil in large saucepan. Turn off heat. Soak cabbage leaves in water 5 minutes; remove, drain and cool.

2. Combine lamb, rice, salt, oregano, nutmeg and pepper in large bowl. Place 2 tablespoonfuls mixture in center of each cabbage leaf; roll firmly. Place cabbage rolls in slow cooker, seam sides down. Pour tomato sauce over cabbage rolls. Cover and cook on LOW 8 to 10 hours.

Slow Roasted Potatoes

Makes 3 to 4 servings

16 small new potatoes
   3 tablespoons butter, cut into ⅛-inch pieces
   1 teaspoon paprika
½ teaspoon salt
¼ teaspoon garlic powder
   Black pepper to taste

Combine all ingredients in slow cooker; mix well. Cover and cook on LOW 7 hours or on HIGH 4 hours. Remove potatoes with slotted spoon to serving dish; cover to keep warm. Add 1 to 2 tablespoons water to drippings and stir until well blended. Pour mixture over potatoes.

Classic Cabbage Rolls

Donna's Potato Casserole

Makes 8 to 10 servings

1 can (10¾ ounces) condensed cream of chicken soup, undiluted
8 ounces sour cream
¼ cup chopped onion
¼ cup plus 3 tablespoons butter, melted and divided
1 teaspoon salt
2 pounds potatoes, peeled and chopped
2 cups shredded Cheddar cheese
1½ to 2 cups stuffing mix

1. Combine soup, sour cream, onion, ¼ cup butter and salt in small bowl.

2. Combine potatoes and cheese in slow cooker. Pour soup mixture into slow cooker; mix well. Sprinkle stuffing mix over potato mixture; drizzle with remaining 3 tablespoons butter. Cover and cook on LOW 8 to 10 hours or on HIGH 5 to 6 hours or until potatoes are tender.

TIP **Store potatoes in a cool, dark, dry, well-ventilated place. Do not refrigerate them. It is important to protect potatoes from light, which can cause them to turn green.**

Donna's Potato Casserole

Boston Brown Bread

Makes 3 loaves

3 (16-ounce) cleaned empty vegetable cans
½ cup rye flour
½ cup yellow cornmeal
½ cup whole-wheat flour
3 tablespoons sugar
1 teaspoon baking soda
¾ teaspoon salt
½ cup chopped walnuts
½ cup raisins
1 cup buttermilk*
⅓ cup molasses

*Soured fresh milk may be substituted. To sour, place 1 tablespoon lemon juice plus enough milk to equal 1 cup in 2-cup measure. Stir; let stand 5 minutes before using.

1. Spray vegetable cans and 1 side of three 6-inch-square pieces heavy-duty aluminum foil with nonstick cooking spray; set aside.

2. Combine rye flour, cornmeal, whole-wheat flour, sugar, baking soda and salt in large bowl. Stir in walnuts and raisins. Whisk buttermilk and molasses in medium bowl until blended. Add buttermilk mixture to dry ingredients; stir until well mixed. Spoon mixture evenly into prepared cans. Place 1 piece of foil, greased side down, on top of each can. Secure foil with rubber bands or cotton string.

3. Place filled cans in slow cooker. Pour boiling water into slow cooker to come halfway up sides of cans. (Make sure foil tops do not touch boiling water.) Cover and cook on LOW 4 hours or until skewer inserted into centers comes out clean. To remove bread, place cans on sides; roll and tap gently on all sides until bread releases. Cool completely on wire racks.

Boston Brown Bread

Spicy Beans Tex-Mex

Makes 8 to 10 servings

⅓ **cup lentils**
1⅓ **cups water**
   5 **strips bacon**
   1 **can (16 ounces) pinto beans, undrained**
   1 **can (16 ounces) red kidney beans, undrained**
   1 **can (15 ounces) diced tomatoes, undrained**
   1 **medium onion, chopped**
   3 **tablespoons ketchup**
   3 **cloves garlic, minced**
   1 **teaspoon chili powder**
 ½ **teaspoon ground cumin**
 ¼ **teaspoon red pepper flakes**
   1 **bay leaf**

1. Boil lentils in water 20 to 30 minutes in large saucepan; drain.

2. In small skillet, cook bacon until crisp; remove, drain and crumble bacon. In same skillet, cook onion in bacon drippings until soft.

3. Combine lentils, bacon, onion, beans, tomatoes with juice, ketchup, garlic, chili powder, cumin, pepper flakes and bay leaf in slow cooker. Cook on HIGH 3 to 4 hours. Remove bay leaf before serving. Garnish as desired.

Spicy Beans Tex-Mex

Swiss Cheese Scalloped Potatoes

Makes 5 to 6 servings

2 pounds baking potatoes, peeled and thinly sliced
½ cup finely chopped yellow onion
¼ teaspoon salt
¼ teaspoon ground nutmeg
2 tablespoons butter, cut into ⅛-inch pieces
½ cup milk
2 tablespoons all-purpose flour
3 ounces Swiss cheese slices, torn into small pieces
¼ cup finely chopped green onions (optional)

1. Layer half the potatoes, ¼ cup onion, ⅛ teaspoon salt, ⅛ teaspoon nutmeg and 1 tablespoon butter in slow cooker. Repeat layers. Cover and cook on LOW 7 hours or on HIGH 4 hours. Remove potatoes with slotted spoon to serving dish.

2. Blend milk and flour in small bowl until smooth. Stir mixture into slow cooker. Add cheese; stir to combine. If slow cooker is on LOW, turn to HIGH; cover and cook until slightly thickened, about 10 minutes. Stir. Pour cheese mixture over potatoes and serve. Garnish with chopped green onions, if desired.

Green Bean Casserole

Makes 4 to 6 servings

2 packages (10 ounces each) frozen green beans, thawed
1 can (10½ ounces) condensed cream of mushroom soup, undiluted
1 tablespoon chopped roasted red peppers
1 tablespoon chopped fresh parsley
1 teaspoon dried sage
½ teaspoon salt
½ teaspoon black pepper
¼ teaspoon ground nutmeg
½ cup toasted almonds, slivered or sliced

Combine all ingredients except almonds in slow cooker. Cover and cook on LOW 3 to 4 hours. Sprinkle with almonds.

Swiss Cheese Scalloped Potatoes

Sweet-Spiced Sweet Potatoes

Makes 4 servings

**2 pounds sweet potatoes, peeled and cut into ½-inch
    pieces
¼ cup packed dark brown sugar
1 teaspoon ground cinnamon
½ teaspoon ground nutmeg
⅛ teaspoon salt
2 tablespoons butter, cut into ⅛-inch pieces
1 teaspoon vanilla**

Combine all ingredients except butter and vanilla in slow cooker; mix well.
Cover and cook on LOW 7 hours or on HIGH 4 hours. Add butter and
vanilla; stir to blend. Garnish as desired.

Skinny Cornbread

Makes 8 servings

**1¼ cups all-purpose flour
¾ cup yellow cornmeal
¼ cup sugar
1 teaspoon baking powder
1 teaspoon baking soda
1 teaspoon seasoned salt
1 cup nonfat buttermilk
¼ cup cholesterol-free egg substitute
¼ cup canola oil**

1. Lightly grease 2-quart soufflé dish; set aside. Place rack or metal trivet in
slow cooker; preheat slow cooker. Sift flour, cornmeal, sugar, baking powder,
baking soda and seasoned salt into large bowl. Make well in center of dry
ingredients. Pour buttermilk, egg substitute and oil into well in dry ingredients;
mix just until moistened.

2. Pour batter into prepared dish; cover with lid or foil. Carefully place on
rack in slow cooker. Cook on HIGH 30 minutes to 2 hours or on LOW 3 to
4 hours or until edges are golden and knife inserted into center comes out
clean. Cook the cornbread with slow cooker lid ajar to allow any condensation
to evaporate.

Sweet-Spiced Sweet Potatoes

Orange-Spice Glazed Carrots

Makes 6 servings

> 1 package (32 ounces) baby carrots
> ½ cup packed light brown sugar
> ½ cup orange juice
> 3 tablespoons butter or margarine
> ¾ teaspoon ground cinnamon
> ¼ teaspoon ground nutmeg
> 2 tablespoons cornstarch
> ¼ cup cold water

1. Combine all ingredients except cornstarch and water in slow cooker. Cover and cook on LOW 3½ to 4 hours or until carrots are crisp-tender.

2. Spoon carrots into serving bowl. Remove juices to small saucepan. Heat to a boil. Mix cornstarch and water in small bowl until blended. Stir into saucepan. Boil 1 minute or until thickened, stirring constantly. Spoon over carrots.

Rustic Garlic Mashed Potatoes

Makes 5 servings

> 2 pounds baking potatoes, unpeeled, cut into ½-inch cubes
> ¼ cup water
> 2 tablespoons butter, cut into ⅛-inch pieces
> 1¼ teaspoons salt
> ½ teaspoon garlic powder
> ¼ teaspoon black pepper
> 1 cup milk

Place all ingredients except milk in slow cooker; toss to combine. Cover and cook on LOW 7 hours or on HIGH 4 hours. Add milk to slow cooker. Mash potatoes with potato masher or electric mixer until smooth.

Orange-Spice Glazed Carrots

Five-Bean Casserole

Susan Richardson ◆ *Portland, OR*

Makes 16 servings

2 medium onions, chopped
8 ounces bacon, diced
2 cloves garlic, minced
½ cup packed brown sugar
½ cup cider vinegar
1 teaspoon salt
1 teaspoon dry mustard
¼ teaspoon black pepper
2 cans (about 16 ounces each) kidney beans, rinsed and drained
1 can (about 16 ounces) chick-peas, rinsed and drained
1 can (about 16 ounces) butter beans, rinsed and drained
1 can (about 16 ounces) Great Northern or cannellini beans, rinsed and drained
1 can (about 16 ounces) baked beans

1. Cook and stir onions, bacon and garlic in large skillet over medium heat until onions are tender; drain. Stir in brown sugar, vinegar, salt, mustard and pepper. Simmer over low heat 15 minutes.

2. Combine beans in slow cooker. Spoon onion mixture evenly over top. Cook on HIGH 3 to 4 hours or on LOW 6 to 8 hours.

Eggplant Italiano

Makes 6 servings

1¼ **pounds eggplant, cut into 1-inch cubes**
  2 **medium onions, thinly sliced**
  2 **ribs celery, cut into 1-inch pieces**
  1 **can (16 ounces) diced tomatoes, undrained**
  3 **tablespoons tomato sauce**
  1 **tablespoon olive oil**
  ½ **cup pitted ripe olives, cut into halves**
  2 **tablespoons balsamic vinegar**
  1 **tablespoon sugar**
  1 **tablespoon capers, drained**
  1 **teaspoon dried oregano or basil leaves**
    Salt and black pepper

1. Combine eggplant, onions, celery, tomatoes with juice, tomato sauce and oil in slow cooker. Cover and cook on LOW 3 ½ to 4 hours or until eggplant is tender.

2. Stir in olives, vinegar, sugar, capers and oregano. Season with salt and pepper to taste. Cover and cook 45 minutes to 1 hour or until heated through. Garnish with fresh basil leaves, leaf lettuce or red jalapeño pepper*, if desired.

*Jalapeño peppers can sting and irritate the skin; wear rubber gloves when handling peppers and do not touch eyes. Wash hands after handling peppers.

Parmesan Potato Wedges

Makes 6 servings

  2 **pounds red potatoes, cut into ½-inch wedges**
  ¼ **cup finely chopped yellow onion**
1½ **teaspoons dried oregano leaves**
  ½ **teaspoon salt**
    Black pepper to taste
  2 **tablespoons butter, cut into ⅛-inch pieces**
  ¼ **cup (1 ounce) grated Parmesan cheese**

Layer potatoes, onion, oregano, salt, pepper and butter in slow cooker. Cook on HIGH 4 hours. Transfer potatoes to serving platter and sprinkle with cheese.

PASTA & RICE

Red Beans and Rice with Ham

Cheryl Hulbert ◆ Newnan, GA

Makes 6 servings

1 package (1 pound) dried red beans
1 pound beef sausage, sliced
1 ham slice, cubed (about 8 ounces)
1 small onion, diced
2½ to 3 cups water
Cayenne pepper to taste
1 teaspoon adobo seasoning with pepper

1. Soak beans overnight; rinse and drain.

2. Place beans in slow cooker. Add sausage, ham, onion and water (3 cups for HIGH; 2½ cups for LOW). Season with cayenne pepper and adobo seasoning.

3. Cover and cook on HIGH 3 to 4 hours or on LOW 7 to 8 hours, stirring every 2 hours, if necessary.

Cheryl says: *Serve over white rice.*

Red Beans and Rice with Ham

Hearty Chili Mac

Makes 4 servings

1 pound lean ground beef
1 can (14½ ounces) diced tomatoes, drained
1 cup chopped onion
1 clove garlic, minced
1 tablespoon chili powder
½ teaspoon salt
½ teaspoon ground cumin
½ teaspoon dried oregano leaves
¼ teaspoon black pepper
¼ teaspoon red pepper flakes
2 cups cooked macaroni

Crumble ground beef into slow cooker. Add remaining ingredients except macaroni to slow cooker. Cover and cook on LOW 4 hours. Stir in cooked macaroni. Cover and cook on LOW 1 hour. Garnish as desired.

Fiesta Rice and Sausage

Makes 10 to 12 servings

1 teaspoon vegetable oil
2 pounds spicy Italian sausage, casing removed
2 cloves garlic, minced
2 teaspoons ground cumin
4 medium onions, chopped
4 medium green bell peppers, chopped
3 jalapeño peppers*, seeded and minced
4 cups beef broth
2 packages (6¼ ounces each) long-grain and wild rice mix

*Jalapeño peppers can sting and irritate the skin; wear rubber gloves when handling peppers and do not touch eyes. Wash hands after handling.

1. Heat oil in large skillet. Brown sausage about 5 minutes, stirring to break up meat. Add garlic and cumin; cook 30 seconds. Add onions, bell peppers and jalapeño peppers. Sauté mixture until onions are tender, about 10 minutes.

2. Pour mixture into slow cooker. Stir in beef broth and rice. Cover and cook on HIGH 1 to 2 hours or on LOW 4 to 6 hours.

Hearty Chili Mac

Shrimp Jambalaya

Lucy Cannek ◆ *Elmhurst, IL*

Makes 6 servings

1 can (28 ounces) diced tomatoes, undrained
1 medium onion, chopped
1 medium red bell pepper, chopped
1 rib celery, chopped (about ½ cup)
2 tablespoons minced garlic
2 teaspoons dried parsley flakes
2 teaspoons dried oregano leaves
1 teaspoon red pepper sauce
½ teaspoon dried thyme leaves
2 pounds large shrimp, cooked, peeled and deveined
2 cups uncooked rice
2 cups fat-free low-sodium chicken broth

1. Combine tomatoes with juice, onion, bell pepper, celery, garlic, parsley, oregano, red pepper sauce and thyme in slow cooker. Cover and cook on LOW 4 hours or on HIGH 8 hours. Stir in shrimp. Cover and cook on LOW 20 minutes.

2. Meanwhile, prepare rice according to package directions, substituting broth for water. Serve jambalaya over hot cooked rice.

Fusilli Pizzaiola with Turkey Meatballs

Makes 4 servings

2 cans (14½ ounces each) no-salt-added tomatoes, undrained
1 can (8 ounces) no-salt-added tomato sauce
¼ cup chopped onion
¼ cup grated carrot
2 tablespoons no-salt-added tomato paste
2 tablespoons chopped fresh basil
1 clove garlic, minced
½ teaspoon dried thyme leaves
¼ teaspoon sugar
¼ teaspoon black pepper, divided
1 bay leaf
1 pound ground turkey breast
1 egg, lightly beaten
1 tablespoon fat-free (skim) milk
¼ cup Italian-seasoned dry bread crumbs
2 tablespoons chopped fresh parsley
8 ounces uncooked fusilli or other spiral-shaped pasta

1. Combine tomatoes with juice, tomato sauce, onion, carrot, tomato paste, basil, garlic, thyme, sugar, ⅛ teaspoon pepper and bay leaf in slow cooker. Break up tomatoes gently with wooden spoon. Cover and cook on LOW 4½ to 5 hours.

2. About 45 minutes before end of cooking, prepare meatballs. Preheat oven to 350°F. Combine turkey, egg and milk; blend in bread crumbs, parsley and remaining ⅛ teaspoon black pepper. With wet hands, shape mixture into small balls. Spray baking sheet with nonstick cooking spray. Arrange meatballs on baking sheet. Bake 25 minutes or until no longer pink in centers.

3. Add meatballs to slow cooker. Cover and cook 45 minutes to 1 hour or until meatballs are heated through. Discard bay leaf.

4. Prepare pasta according to package directions; drain. Place in serving bowl; top with meatballs and sauce.

Tuscan Pasta

Makes 8 servings

1 pound boneless skinless chicken breasts, cut into 1-inch pieces
2 cans (14½ ounces each) Italian-style stewed tomatoes
1 can (15½ ounces) red kidney beans, rinsed and drained
1 can (15 ounces) tomato sauce
1 jar (4½ ounces) sliced mushrooms, drained
1 medium green bell pepper, chopped
1 cup water
½ cup chopped onion
½ cup chopped celery
4 cloves garlic, minced
1 teaspoon dried Italian seasoning
6 ounces uncooked thin spaghetti, broken in half

1. Place all ingredients except spaghetti in slow cooker. Cover and cook on LOW 4 hours or until vegetables are tender.

2. Turn slow cooker to HIGH. Stir in spaghetti; cover. Stir again after 10 minutes. Cover and cook 45 minutes or until pasta is tender. Garnish with basil and bell pepper strips, if desired.

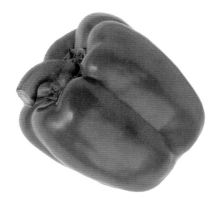

Tuscan Pasta

Slow Cooker Chicken & Rice

Tami Stapleton ◆ *Darlington, SC*

Makes 4 servings

**3 cans (10¾ ounces each) condensed cream of
   chicken soup, undiluted**
2 cups quick-cooking rice
1 cup water
**1 pound boneless, skinless chicken breasts or breast
   tenders**
   Salt and black pepper
   Paprika
½ cup diced celery

Combine soup, rice and water in slow cooker. Add chicken; sprinkle with salt, pepper and paprika. Sprinkle celery over top of chicken. Cover and cook on HIGH 3 to 4 hours or on LOW 6 to 8 hours.

Pesto Rice and Beans

Makes 8 servings

**1 can (15 ounces) Great Northern beans, rinsed and
   drained**
1 can (14 ounces) chicken broth
¾ cup uncooked long-grain white rice
1½ cups frozen cut green beans, thawed and drained
½ cup prepared pesto
   Grated Parmesan cheese (optional)

1. Combine Great Northern beans, chicken broth and rice in slow cooker. Cover and cook on LOW 2 hours.

2. Stir in green beans; cover and cook 1 hour or until rice and beans are tender. Turn off slow cooker and remove insert to heatproof surface. Stir in pesto and Parmesan cheese, if desired. Let stand, covered, 5 minutes or until cheese is melted. Serve immediately.

High

Slow Cooker Chicken & Rice

Spanish-Style Couscous

Makes 4 servings

1 pound lean ground beef
1 can (about 14 ounces) beef broth
1 small green bell pepper, cut into ½-inch pieces
½ cup pimiento-stuffed green olives, sliced
½ medium onion, chopped
2 cloves garlic, minced
1 teaspoon ground cumin
½ teaspoon dried thyme leaves
1⅓ cups water
1 cup uncooked couscous

1. Heat skillet over high heat until hot. Add beef; cook until browned. Drain off fat.

2. Place broth, bell pepper, olives, onion, garlic, cumin, thyme and beef in slow cooker. Cover and cook on LOW 4 hours or until bell pepper is tender.

3. Bring water to a boil in small saucepan over high heat. Stir in couscous. Cover; remove from heat. Let stand 5 minutes; fluff with fork. Spoon couscous onto plates; top with beef mixture. Garnish as desired.

Spanish-Style Couscous

Risi Bisi

Makes 6 servings

1½ cups converted long-grain white rice
¾ cup chopped onion
2 cloves garlic, minced
2 cans (about 14 ounces each) reduced-sodium chicken
　　broth
⅓ cup water
¾ teaspoon dried Italian seasoning
½ teaspoon dried basil leaves
½ cup frozen peas, thawed
¼ cup grated Parmesan cheese
¼ cup toasted pine nuts (optional)

Combine rice, onion and garlic in slow cooker. Heat broth and water to a boil in small saucepan. Stir boiling liquid, Italian seasoning and basil into rice mixture. Cover and cook on LOW 2 to 3 hours or until liquid is absorbed. Add peas. Cover and cook 1 hour. Stir in cheese. Spoon rice into serving bowl. Sprinkle with pine nuts, if desired.

Caribbean Shrimp with Rice

Makes 4 servings

1 package (12 ounces) frozen shrimp, thawed
½ cup chicken broth
1 clove garlic, minced
1 teaspoon chili powder
½ teaspoon salt
½ teaspoon dried oregano leaves
1 cup frozen peas
½ cup diced tomatoes
2 cups cooked rice

Combine shrimp, broth, garlic, chili powder, salt and oregano in slow cooker. Cover and cook on LOW 2 hours. Add peas and tomatoes. Cover and cook on LOW 5 minutes. Stir in rice. Cover and cook on LOW an additional 5 minutes.

Risi Bisi

Easy Beef Stroganoff

Mary Braam ◆ *Raleigh, NC*

Makes 4 to 6 servings

**3 cans (10¾ ounces each) condensed cream of chicken
  soup or condensed cream of mushroom soup,
  undiluted
1 cup sour cream
½ cup water
1 envelope (1 ounce) dried onion soup mix
2 pounds beef stew meat, cubed**

Combine soup, sour cream, water and onion soup mix in slow cooker. Add beef; stir until well coated. Cover and cook on HIGH 3 hours or on LOW 6 hours.

Mary says: *Serve over rice or noodles with a salad and hot bread. You can reduce the calories and fat by using 98% fat-free soup and fat-free sour cream.*

Hungarian Lamb Goulash

Makes 6 servings

**1 package (16 ounces) frozen cut green beans
1 cup chopped onion
1¼ pounds lean lamb stew meat, cut into 1-inch pieces
1 can (15 ounces) chunky tomato sauce
1¾ cups reduced-sodium chicken broth
1 can (6 ounces) tomato paste
4 teaspoons paprika
3 cups hot cooked noodles**

Place green beans and onion in slow cooker. Top with lamb. Combine remaining ingredients except noodles in large bowl; mix well. Pour over lamb mixture. Cover and cook on LOW 6 to 8 hours. Stir. Serve over noodles.

Easy Beef Stroganoff

Veggie Mac and Tuna

Makes 6 servings

1½ cups (6 ounces) elbow macaroni
　3 tablespoons butter or margarine
　1 small onion, chopped
　½ medium red bell pepper, chopped
　½ medium green bell pepper, chopped
　¼ cup all-purpose flour
1¾ cups milk
　8 ounces cubed light pasteurized process cheese product
　½ teaspoon dried marjoram leaves
　1 package (10 ounces) frozen peas
　1 can (9 ounces) tuna in water, drained

1. Cook macaroni according to package directions until just tender; drain.

2. Melt butter in medium saucepan over medium heat. Add onion and bell peppers. Cook and stir 5 minutes or until tender. Add flour. Stir constantly over medium heat 2 minutes. Stir in milk and bring to a boil. Boil, stirring constantly, until thickened. Reduce heat to low; add cheese and marjoram. Stir until cheese is melted.

3. Combine macaroni, cheese sauce, peas and tuna in slow cooker. Cover and cook on LOW 2½ hours or until bubbly at edge.

Veggie Mac and Tuna

Chicken Sausage Pilaf

Makes 4 servings

1 tablespoon vegetable oil
1 pound chicken or turkey sausage, casing removed
1 cup uncooked rice and pasta mix
4 cups chicken broth
2 ribs celery, diced
¼ cup slivered almonds
   Salt and black pepper to taste

Heat oil in large skillet; add sausage. Break up sausage with back of spoon while cooking; cook until browned, about 5 minutes. Add rice and pasta mix to skillet. Cook 1 minute. Place mixture in slow cooker. Add remaining ingredients to slow cooker; stir well. Cover and cook on LOW 7 to 10 hours or on HIGH 3 to 4 hours or until rice is tender. Garnish as desired.

Easy Dirty Rice

Makes 4 servings

½ pound Italian sausage or turkey Italian sausage
1 large onion, finely chopped
1 large green bell pepper, finely chopped
2 cups water
1 cup uncooked long-grain rice
½ cup finely chopped celery
1½ teaspoons salt
½ teaspoon ground red pepper
½ cup chopped fresh parsley

Remove casing from sausage. Cook sausage in skillet, stirring to break up meat, until no longer pink. Place cooked sausage in slow cooker. Add all remaining ingredients except parsley. Stir to combine. Cover and cook on LOW 2 hours or until rice is tender. Stir in parsley.

Chicken Sausage Pilaf

Broccoli and Beef Pasta

Makes 4 servings

**2 cups broccoli florets *or* 1 package (10 ounces) frozen
  broccoli, thawed**
1 onion, thinly sliced
½ teaspoon dried basil leaves
½ teaspoon dried oregano leaves
½ teaspoon dried thyme leaves
1 can (14½ ounces) Italian-style diced tomatoes, undrained
¾ cup beef broth
1 pound lean ground beef
2 cloves garlic, minced
2 tablespoons tomato paste
2 cups cooked rotini pasta
**3 ounces shredded Cheddar cheese or grated Parmesan
  cheese plus additional for garnish**

1. Layer broccoli, onion, basil, oregano, thyme, tomatoes with juice and broth in slow cooker. Cover and cook on LOW 2½ hours.

2. Combine beef and garlic in large nonstick skillet. Cook over high heat 6 to 8 minutes or until meat is no longer pink, stirring to break up meat; drain. Add beef mixture to slow cooker. Cover and cook 2 hours.

3. Stir in tomato paste. Add pasta and cheese. Cover and cook 30 minutes or until cheese melts and mixture is heated through. Garnish with additional cheese, if desired.

Broccoli and Beef Pasta

1-2-3-4 Chili

Carol Mason ◆ *Hanover Park, IL*

Makes 8 servings

2 pounds ground beef, browned and drained of fat
4 cans (8 ounces each) tomato sauce
3 cans (15 ounces each) chili-spiced kidney beans

Combine all ingredients in slow cooker. Cook on LOW 6 to 8 hours. Garnish with cheese and sliced green onion, if desired.

Carol says: *Just dump everything into your slow cooker. I set mine before going to work and come home to a batch of (cheater) chili! Tastes great with cornbread.*

TIP **Pinto beans are interchangeable with kidney beans in most chili recipes. Both bean types are available dried or canned.**

1-2-3-4 Chili

Clam Chowder

Karen Bassett ◆ *Citrus Heights, CA*

Makes 10 servings

5 cans (10¾ ounces each) low-fat condensed cream of
    potato soup, undiluted
2 cans (12 ounces each) evaporated skim milk
2 cans (10 ounces each) whole clams, rinsed and drained
1 can (14¾ ounces) cream-style corn
2 cans (4 ounces each) tiny shrimp, rinsed and drained
¾ cup crumbled bacon (about ½ pound) or imitation bacon
    bits
    Lemon pepper to taste
    Oyster crackers

Combine all ingredients except crackers in slow cooker. Cover and cook on
LOW 3 to 4 hours, stirring occasionally. Serve with oyster crackers.

Campfire Sausage and Potato Soup

Makes 6 to 7 servings

1 can (15½ ounces) dark kidney beans, rinsed and drained
1 can (14½ ounces) diced tomatoes, undrained
1 can (10½ ounces) condensed beef broth, undiluted
8 ounces kielbasa sausage, cut lengthwise into halves,
    then crosswise into ½-inch pieces
1 large baking potato, cut into ½-inch cubes
1 medium green bell pepper, diced
1 medium onion, diced
1 teaspoon dried oregano leaves
½ teaspoon sugar
1 to 2 teaspoons ground cumin

Combine all ingredients except cumin in slow cooker. Cover and cook on
LOW 8 hours or on HIGH 4 hours. Stir in cumin; serve.

Clam Chowder

Vegetable Medley Soup

Makes 12 servings

3 medium sweet potatoes, peeled and chopped
3 medium zucchini, chopped
2 cups chopped broccoli
1 medium onion, chopped
¼ cup butter, melted
3 cans (about 14 ounces each) chicken broth
2 medium white potatoes, peeled and shredded
1 rib celery, finely chopped
1 tablespoon salt
1 teaspoon ground cumin
1 teaspoon black pepper
2 cups half-and-half or milk

Combine sweet potatoes, zucchini, broccoli, onion and butter in large bowl. Add chicken broth; stir. Add white potatoes, celery, salt, cumin and pepper; stir. Pour mixture into slow cooker. Cover and cook on LOW 8 to 10 hours or on HIGH 4 to 5 hours. Add half-and-half; cook 30 minutes to 1 hour. Garnish as desired.

Vegetable Medley Soup

Hamburger Soup

Scarlet Waxman ◆ *Orlando, FL*

Makes 6 to 8 servings

1 pound lean ground beef
1 envelope (1 ounce) dried onion soup mix
1 envelope (1 ounce) Italian seasoning mix
¼ teaspoon seasoned salt
¼ teaspoon black pepper
3 cups boiling water
1 can (8 ounces) diced tomatoes, undrained
1 can (8 ounces) tomato sauce
1 tablespoon soy sauce
1 cup sliced celery
1 cup thinly sliced carrots
2 cups cooked macaroni
¼ cup grated Parmesan cheese
2 tablespoons chopped fresh parsley

1. Brown beef in medium skillet over medium-high heat; drain. Add beef to slow cooker. Add soup mix, Italian seasoning, seasoned salt and pepper. Stir in water, tomatoes with juice, tomato sauce and soy sauce. Add celery and carrots. Cover and cook on LOW 6 to 8 hours.

2. Increase to HIGH; stir in cooked macaroni and Parmesan cheese. Cover and cook 10 to 15 minutes. Sprinkle with parsley just before serving.

Hamburger Soup

Classic French Onion Soup

Makes 4 servings

¼ cup butter
3 large yellow onions, sliced
1 cup dry white wine
3 cans (about 14 ounces each) beef or chicken broth
1 teaspoon Worcestershire sauce
½ teaspoon salt
½ teaspoon dried thyme leaves
1 loaf French bread, sliced and toasted
1 cup (4 ounces) shredded Swiss cheese
Fresh thyme sprig for garnish

1. Melt butter in large skillet over high heat. Add onions; cook and stir 15 minutes or until onions are soft and lightly browned. Stir in wine.

2. Combine onion mixture, beef broth, Worcestershire, salt and thyme in slow cooker. Cover and cook on LOW 4 to 4½ hours. Ladle soup into 4 individual bowls; top with bread slices and cheese. Garnish with fresh thyme, if desired.

Double Thick Baked Potato-Cheese Soup

Makes 7 servings

2 pounds baking potatoes, peeled and cut into ½-inch cubes
2 cans (10½ ounces each) cream of mushroom soup, undiluted
1½ cups finely chopped green onions, divided
¼ teaspoon garlic powder
⅛ teaspoon ground red pepper
1½ cups (6 ounces) shredded sharp Cheddar cheese
1 cup (8 ounces) sour cream
1 cup milk
Black pepper

Combine potatoes, soup, 1 cup green onions, garlic powder and red pepper in slow cooker. Cover and cook on HIGH 4 hours or on LOW 8 hours. Add cheese, sour cream and milk; stir until cheese is completely melted. Cover and cook on HIGH an additional 10 minutes. Season to taste with black pepper. Garnish with remaining ½ cup green onions.

Classic French Onion Soup

Slow Cooker Cheese Soup

Makes 4 servings

2 cans (10¾ ounces each) condensed cream of celery soup, undiluted
1 pound Cheddar cheese, shredded
1 teaspoon paprika
1 teaspoon Worcestershire sauce
1¼ cups half-and-half
Salt and black pepper

Combine first four ingredients in slow cooker. Cover and cook on LOW 2 to 3 hours. Add half-and-half; stir to combine. Cover and cook another 20 minutes. Season with salt and pepper to taste. Garnish as desired.

Navy Bean Bacon Chowder

Makes 6 servings

1½ cups dried navy beans, rinsed and drained
2 cups cold water
6 slices thick-cut bacon
1 medium carrot, cut lengthwise into halves, then cut into 1-inch pieces
1 rib celery, chopped
1 medium onion, chopped
1 small turnip, cut into 1-inch pieces
1 teaspoon dried Italian seasoning
⅛ teaspoon black pepper
1 large can (46 ounces) reduced-sodium chicken broth
1 cup milk

1. Soak beans overnight in cold water.

2. Cook bacon in medium skillet over medium heat. Drain and crumble. Combine carrot, celery, onion, turnip, Italian seasoning, pepper, beans and bacon in slow cooker; mix slightly. Pour broth over top. Cover and cook on LOW 7½ to 9 hours or until beans are crisp-tender. Ladle 2 cups of soup mixture into food processor or blender. Process until smooth; return to slow cooker. Add milk; cover and heat on HIGH 10 minutes or until heated through.

Slow Cooker Cheese Soup

Vegetarian Chili

Makes 4 servings

1 tablespoon vegetable oil
1 cup finely chopped onion
1 cup chopped red bell pepper
2 tablespoons minced jalapeño pepper*
1 clove garlic, minced
1 can (28 ounces) crushed tomatoes
1 can (14½ ounces) black beans, rinsed and drained
1 can (14 ounces) garbanzo beans, rinsed and drained
½ cup canned corn
¼ cup tomato paste
1 teaspoon sugar
1 teaspoon ground cumin
1 teaspoon dried basil leaves
1 teaspoon chili powder
¼ teaspoon black pepper
Sour cream (optional)
1 cup shredded Cheddar cheese (optional)

*Jalapeño peppers can sting and irritate the skin; wear rubber gloves when handling peppers and do not touch eyes. Wash hands after handling.

1. Heat oil in large nonstick skillet over medium-high heat until hot. Add onion, bell pepper, jalapeño pepper and garlic; cook and stir 5 minutes or until vegetables are tender.

2. Spoon vegetables into slow cooker. Add remaining ingredients except sour cream and cheese to slow cooker; mix well. Cover and cook on LOW 4 to 5 hours. Garnish with sour cream and cheese, if desired.

Vegetarian Chili

Chicken and Vegetable Chowder

Makes 6 servings

1 pound boneless skinless chicken breasts, cut into 1-inch pieces
1 can (14½ ounces) reduced-sodium chicken broth
1 can (10¾ ounces) condensed cream of potato soup, undiluted
10 ounces frozen broccoli cuts
1 cup sliced carrots
1 jar (4½ ounces) sliced mushrooms, drained
½ cup chopped onion
½ cup whole kernel corn
2 cloves garlic, minced
½ teaspoon dried thyme leaves
⅓ cup half-and-half

Combine all ingredients except half-and-half in slow cooker. Cover and cook on LOW 5 hours or until vegetables are tender and chicken is no longer pink in center. Stir in half-and-half. Turn to HIGH. Cover and cook 15 minutes or until heated through.

Variation: Add ½ cup (2 ounces) shredded Swiss or Cheddar cheese to thickened broth and half-and-half, if desired. Stir over LOW heat until melted.

Chicken and Vegetable Chowder

Chili with Beans and Corn

Makes 6 to 8 servings

1 (16-ounce) can black-eyed peas or cannellini beans, rinsed and drained
1 (16-ounce) can kidney or navy beans, rinsed and drained
1 (15-ounce) can whole tomatoes, drained and chopped
1 cup corn
1 cup water
1 medium onion, chopped
½ cup chopped green onions
½ cup tomato paste
¼ cup diced jalapeño peppers*
1 tablespoon chili powder
1 teaspoon ground cumin
1 teaspoon mustard
½ teaspoon dried oregano leaves

*Jalapeño peppers can sting and irritate the skin; wear rubber gloves when handling peppers and do not touch eyes. Wash hands after handling.

Combine all ingredients in slow cooker. Cover and cook on LOW 8 to 10 hours or on HIGH 4 to 5 hours. Garnish as desired.

Chili with Beans and Corn

Mediterranean Shrimp Soup

Makes 6 servings

2 cans (14½ ounces each) reduced-sodium chicken broth
**1 can (14½ ounces) whole tomatoes, undrained, coarsely
  chopped**
1 can (8 ounces) tomato sauce
1 medium onion, chopped
½ medium green bell pepper, chopped
1 jar (2½ ounces) sliced mushrooms
½ cup orange juice
½ cup dry white wine (optional)
¼ cup ripe olives, sliced
2 cloves garlic, minced
2 bay leaves
1 teaspoon dried basil leaves
¼ teaspoon fennel seed, crushed
⅛ teaspoon black pepper
1 pound medium shrimp, peeled

Place all ingredients except shrimp in slow cooker. Cover and cook on LOW 4 to 4½ hours or until vegetables are crisp-tender. Stir in shrimp. Cover and cook 15 to 30 minutes or until shrimp are opaque. Remove and discard bay leaves.

Hint: For a heartier soup, add fish. Cut 1 pound of whitefish or cod into 1-inch pieces. Add to slow cooker 45 minutes before serving. Cover and cook on LOW.

Mediterranean Shrimp Soup

Savory Pea Soup with Sausage

Makes 6 servings

**8 ounces smoked sausage, cut lengthwise into halves,
    then cut into ½-inch pieces
1 package (16 ounces) dried split peas, sorted and rinsed
3 medium carrots, sliced
2 ribs celery, sliced
1 medium onion, chopped
¾ teaspoon dried marjoram leaves
1 bay leaf
2 cans (14½ ounces each) reduced-sodium chicken broth**

Heat small skillet over medium heat. Add sausage; cook 5 to 8 minutes or until browned. Drain well. Combine sausage and remaining ingredients in slow cooker. Cover and cook on LOW 4 to 5 hours or until peas are tender. Turn off heat. Remove and discard bay leaf. Cover and let stand 15 minutes to thicken.

Country Chicken Chowder

Makes 8 servings

**2 tablespoons margarine or butter
1½ pounds chicken tenders, cut into ½-inch pieces
2 cups frozen corn
2 small onions, chopped
2 ribs celery, sliced
2 small carrots, sliced
2 cans (10¾ ounces each) condensed cream of potato
    soup, undiluted
1½ cups chicken broth
1 teaspoon dried dill weed
½ cup half-and-half**

1. Melt margarine in large skillet. Add chicken; cook until browned.

2. Add cooked chicken, corn, onions, celery, carrots, soup, chicken broth and dill to slow cooker. Cover and cook on LOW 3 to 4 hours or until chicken is no longer pink and vegetables are tender. Turn off heat; stir in half-and-half. Cover and let stand 5 to 10 minutes or until heated through.

Note: For a special touch, garnish soup with croutons and fresh dill.

Savory Pea Soup with Sausage

Chili with Chocolate

Shawna Steffen ◆ *Willmar, MN*

Makes 4 servings

1 pound ground beef
1 medium onion, chopped
3 cloves garlic, minced, divided
1 can (28 ounces) diced tomatoes, undrained
1 can (15 ounces) chili beans
1½ tablespoons chili powder
1½ teaspoons cumin
1 tablespoon grated semisweet baking chocolate
　　Hot pepper sauce
　　Salt
　　Black pepper

1. Brown ground beef, onion and 1 clove garlic in large nonstick skillet over medium-low heat. Drain off fat.

2. Place meat mixture in slow cooker. Add remaining ingredients, including 2 cloves garlic; mix well. Cover and cook on LOW 5 to 6 hours. Garnish as desired.

Chili with Chocolate

Creamy Turkey Soup

Makes 5 to 6 servings

2 cans (10¾ ounces each) cream of chicken soup, undiluted
2 cups chopped cooked turkey breast
1 package (8 ounces) sliced mushrooms
1 medium yellow onion, chopped
1 teaspoon rubbed sage *or* ½ teaspoon dried poultry
**   seasoning**
1 cup frozen peas, thawed
½ cup milk
1 jar (about 4 ounces) diced pimiento

1. Combine soup, turkey, mushrooms, onion and sage in slow cooker. Cook on LOW 8 hours or on HIGH 4 hours.

2. If cooking on LOW, turn to HIGH; stir in peas, milk and pimiento pieces. Cook an additional 10 minutes or until heated through.

Turkey-Tomato Soup

Makes 6 servings

2 medium turkey thighs, boned, skinned and cut into
**   1-inch pieces**
2 small white or red potatoes, cubed
1¾ cups fat-free reduced-sodium chicken broth
1½ cups frozen corn
1 cup chopped onion
1 cup water
1 can (8 ounces) no-salt-added tomato sauce
¼ cup tomato paste
2 tablespoons Dijon mustard
1 teaspoon hot pepper sauce
½ teaspoon sugar
½ teaspoon garlic powder
¼ cup finely chopped fresh parsley

Combine all ingredients except parsley in slow cooker. Cover and cook on LOW 9 to 10 hours. Stir in parsley before serving.

Creamy Turkey Soup

Fiesta Black Bean Soup

Makes 6 to 8 servings

6 cups chicken broth
¾ pound potatoes, peeled and diced
1 can (16 ounces) black beans, rinsed and drained
½ pound ham, diced
½ medium onion, diced
1 can (4 ounces) chopped jalapeño peppers*
2 teaspoons dried oregano leaves
1½ teaspoons dried thyme leaves
2 cloves garlic, minced
1 teaspoon ground cumin
Sour cream, chopped bell peppers and chopped tomatoes, for garnish

*Jalapeño peppers can sting and irritate the skin; wear rubber gloves when handling peppers and do not touch eyes. Wash hands after handling.

Combine all ingredients except garnish in slow cooker. Cover and cook on LOW 8 to 10 hours or on HIGH 4 to 5 hours. Garnish, if desired.

Tuscan White Bean Soup

Makes 8 to 10 servings

6 ounces smoked bacon, diced
10 cups chicken broth
1 bag (16 ounces) dried Great Northern beans, rinsed and drained
1 can (14½ ounces) diced tomatoes, undrained
1 large onion, chopped
3 carrots, peeled and chopped
4 cloves garlic, minced
1 fresh rosemary sprig *or* 1 teaspoon dried rosemary leaves
1 teaspoon black pepper

Cook bacon in medium skillet until just golden; drain. Transfer bacon to slow cooker. Add remaining ingredients. Cover and cook on LOW 8 hours or until beans are tender. Remove rosemary sprig before serving.

Serving Suggestion: Place slices of toasted Italian bread in bottoms of individual soup bowls. Drizzle with olive oil. Pour soup over bread and serve.

Fiesta Black Bean Soup

HEARTY STEWS

Favorite Beef Stew

Makes 6 to 8 servings

3 carrots, cut lengthwise into halves, then cut into 1-inch pieces
3 ribs celery, cut into 1-inch pieces
2 large potatoes, peeled and cut into ½-inch pieces
1½ cups chopped onions
3 cloves garlic, chopped
1 bay leaf
4½ teaspoons Worcestershire sauce
¾ teaspoon dried thyme leaves
¾ teaspoon dried basil leaves
½ teaspoon black pepper
2 pounds lean beef stew meat, cut into 1-inch pieces
1 can (14½ ounces) diced tomatoes, undrained
1 can (about 14 ounces) reduced-sodium beef broth
½ cup cold water
¼ cup all-purpose flour

1. Layer ingredients in slow cooker in the following order: carrots, celery, potatoes, onions, garlic, bay leaf, Worcestershire, thyme, basil, pepper, beef, tomatoes with juice and broth. Cover and cook on LOW 8 to 9 hours.

2. Remove beef and vegetables to large serving bowl; cover and keep warm. Remove and discard bay leaf. Turn slow cooker to HIGH; cover.

3. Stir water into flour in small bowl until smooth. Add ½ cup cooking liquid; mix well. Stir flour mixture into slow cooker. Cover and cook 15 minutes or until thickened. Pour sauce over meat and vegetables. Serve immediately.

Favorite Beef Stew

Hearty Lentil Stew

Makes 6 servings

1 cup dried lentils, rinsed and drained
1 package (16 ounces) frozen green beans
2 cups cauliflower florets
1 cup chopped onion
1 cup baby carrots, cut in half crosswise
3 cups fat-free reduced-sodium chicken broth
2 teaspoons ground cumin
¾ teaspoon ground ginger
1 can (15 ounces) chunky tomato sauce with garlic and herbs
½ cup dry-roasted peanuts

Place lentils in slow cooker. Top with green beans, cauliflower, onion and carrots. Combine broth, cumin and ginger in large bowl; mix well. Pour mixture over vegetables. Cover and cook on LOW 9 to 11 hours. Stir in tomato sauce. Cover and cook on LOW 10 minutes. Sprinkle peanuts onto individual servings.

Irish Stew

Makes 6 servings

1 cup fat-free reduced-sodium chicken broth
1 teaspoon dried marjoram leaves
1 teaspoon dried parsley leaves
¾ teaspoon salt
½ teaspoon garlic powder
¼ teaspoon black pepper
1¼ pounds white potatoes, peeled and cut into 1-inch pieces
1 pound lean lamb stew meat, cut into 1-inch cubes
1½ cups coarsely chopped carrots
8 ounces frozen cut green beans
2 small leeks, cut lengthwise into halves, then crosswise into slices

Combine broth, marjoram, parsley, salt, garlic powder and pepper in large bowl; mix well. Pour mixture into slow cooker. Add potatoes, lamb, carrots, green beans and leeks. Cover and cook on LOW 7 to 9 hours.

Hearty Lentil Stew

Pork and Mushroom Ragoût

Makes 6 servings

> Nonstick cooking spray
> 1 boneless pork loin roast (1¼ pounds)
> 1¼ cups canned crushed tomatoes, divided
> 2 tablespoons cornstarch
> 2 teaspoons dried savory leaves
> 3 sun-dried tomatoes, patted dry and chopped
> 1 package (8 ounces) sliced mushrooms
> 1 large onion, sliced
> 1 teaspoon black pepper
> 3 cups hot cooked noodles

1. Spray large nonstick skillet with cooking spray; heat over medium heat until hot. Brown roast on all sides; set aside.

2. Combine ½ cup crushed tomatoes, cornstarch, savory and sun-dried tomatoes in large bowl. Pour mixture into slow cooker. Layer mushrooms, onion and roast over tomato mixture.

3. Pour remaining ¾ cup tomatoes over roast; sprinkle with pepper. Cover and cook on LOW 4 to 6 hours or until internal temperature reaches 165°F when tested with meat thermometer inserted into thickest part of roast.

4. Remove roast from slow cooker. Transfer roast to cutting board; cover with foil. Let stand 10 to 15 minutes before slicing. Internal temperature will continue to rise 5° to 10°F during stand time. Serve over hot cooked noodles.

Pork and Mushroom Ragoût

Mushroom-Beef Stew

Dana R. Moore ◆ *Rochester, NY*

Makes 4 servings

1 pound beef stew meat
1 can (10¾ ounces) cream of mushroom soup, undiluted
1 envelope (1 ounce) dry onion soup mix
2 cans (4 ounces each) sliced mushrooms, drained

Combine all ingredients in slow cooker. Cover and cook on LOW 8 to 10 hours.

Dana says: *Serve over hot cooked rice or noodles.*

Chicken and Chili Pepper Stew

Makes 6 servings

1 pound boneless skinless chicken thighs, cut into ½-inch pieces
1 pound small potatoes, cut lengthwise into halves, then crosswise into slices
1 cup chopped onion
2 poblano chili peppers, seeded and cut into ½-inch pieces
1 jalapeño pepper,* seeded and finely chopped
3 cloves garlic, minced
3 cups fat-free reduced-sodium chicken broth
1 can (14½ ounces) no-salt-added diced tomatoes, undrained
2 tablespoons chili powder
1 teaspoon dried oregano leaves

Jalapeño peppers can sting and irritate the skin; wear rubber gloves when handling peppers and do not touch eyes. Wash hands after handling.

1. Place chicken, potatoes, onion, poblano peppers, jalapeño pepper and garlic in slow cooker.

2. Stir together broth, tomatoes with juice, chili powder and oregano in large bowl. Pour broth mixture over chicken mixture in slow cooker; stir. Cover and cook on LOW 8 to 9 hours.

Mushroom-Beef Stew

Stew Provençal

Makes 8 servings

2 cans (about 14 ounces each) beef broth, divided
⅓ cup all-purpose flour
1½ pounds pork tenderloin, trimmed and diced
4 red potatoes, unpeeled and cut into cubes
2 cups frozen cut green beans
1 medium onion, chopped
2 cloves garlic, minced
1 teaspoon salt
1 teaspoon dried thyme leaves
½ teaspoon black pepper

1. Combine ¾ cup beef broth and flour in small bowl. Set aside.

2. Add remaining broth, pork, potatoes, beans, onion, garlic, salt, thyme and pepper to slow cooker; stir. Cover and cook on LOW 8 to 10 hours or on HIGH 4 to 5 hours. If cooking on LOW, turn to HIGH last 30 minutes. Stir in flour mixture. Cook 30 minutes to thicken.

Italian Sausage and Vegetable Stew

Makes 6 (1-cup) servings

1 pound hot or mild Italian sausage, cut into 1-inch pieces
1 package (16 ounces) frozen mixed vegetables (onions and green, red and yellow bell peppers)
1 can (14½ ounces) diced Italian-style tomatoes, undrained
2 medium zucchini, sliced
1 jar (4½ ounces) sliced mushrooms, drained
4 cloves garlic, minced
2 tablespoons Italian-style tomato paste

1. Heat large skillet over high heat until hot. Add sausage; cook about 5 minutes or until browned. Pour off any drippings.

2. Combine sausage, frozen vegetables, tomatoes with juice, zucchini, mushrooms and garlic in slow cooker. Cover and cook on LOW 4 to 4½ hours or until zucchini is tender. Stir in tomato paste. Cover and cook 30 minutes or until thickened.

Stew Provençal

The Best Beef Stew

Makes 8 servings

½ cup plus 2 tablespoons all-purpose flour, divided
2 teaspoons salt
1 teaspoon black pepper
3 pounds beef stew meat, trimmed and cut into cubes
3 medium potatoes, peeled and diced
1 can (16 ounces) diced tomatoes in juice, undrained
4 ribs celery, sliced
½ pound smoked sausage, sliced
1 cup chopped leek
1 cup chopped onion
½ cup chicken broth
3 cloves garlic, minced
1 teaspoon dried thyme leaves
3 tablespoons water

1. Combine ½ cup flour, salt and pepper in large resealable plastic food storage bag. Add beef; shake bag to coat beef. Place beef in slow cooker. Add remaining ingredients except remaining 2 tablespoons flour and water; stir well. Cover and cook on LOW 8 to 12 hours or on HIGH 4 to 6 hours.

2. One hour before serving, turn slow cooker to HIGH. Combine remaining 2 tablespoons flour and water in small bowl; stir until mixture becomes paste. Stir mixture into slow cooker; mix well. Cover and cook until thickened. Garnish as desired before serving.

The Best Beef Stew

Russian Borscht

Makes 12 servings

4 cups thinly sliced green cabbage
1½ pounds fresh beets, shredded
5 small carrots, peeled, cut lengthwise into halves, then cut into 1-inch pieces
1 parsnip, peeled, cut lengthwise into halves, then cut into 1-inch pieces
1 cup chopped onion
4 cloves garlic, minced
1 pound lean beef stew meat, cut into ½-inch cubes
1 can (14½ ounces) diced tomatoes, undrained
3 cans (about 14 ounces each) reduced-sodium beef broth
¼ cup lemon juice
1 tablespoon sugar
1 teaspoon black pepper
Sour cream (optional)
Fresh parsley (optional)

Layer ingredients in slow cooker in the following order: cabbage, beets, carrots, parsnip, onion, garlic, beef, tomatoes with juice, broth, lemon juice, sugar and pepper. Cover and cook on LOW 7 to 9 hours or until vegetables are crisp-tender. Season with additional lemon juice and sugar, if desired. Dollop with sour cream and garnish with parsley, if desired.

TIP **Look for deep, rich purple-red beets that are firm with smooth skins and tops attached. Beet tops should be fresh looking and dark green, not wilted or slimy. Also, small and medium-sized beets are usually sweeter and more tender.**

Russian Borscht

Mediterranean Stew

Makes 6 servings

1 medium butternut or acorn squash, peeled and cut into 1-inch cubes
2 cups unpeeled eggplant, cut into 1-inch cubes
2 cups sliced zucchini
1 can (15½ ounces) chick-peas, rinsed and drained
1 package (10 ounces) frozen cut okra
1 can (8 ounces) tomato sauce
1 cup chopped onion
1 medium tomato, chopped
1 medium carrot, thinly sliced
½ cup reduced-sodium vegetable broth
⅓ cup raisins
1 clove garlic, minced
½ teaspoon ground cumin
½ teaspoon ground turmeric
¼ to ½ teaspoon ground red pepper
¼ teaspoon ground cinnamon
¼ teaspoon paprika
6 to 8 cups hot cooked couscous or rice
Fresh parsley (optional)

Combine all ingredients except couscous and parsley in slow cooker; mix well. Cover and cook on LOW 8 to 10 hours or until vegetables are crisp-tender. Serve over couscous. Garnish with parsley, if desired.

Mediterranean Stew

Turkey Mushroom Stew

Makes 4 servings

1 pound turkey cutlets, cut into 4×1-inch strips
1 small onion, thinly sliced
2 tablespoons minced green onion with top
½ pound mushrooms, sliced
2 to 3 tablespoons all-purpose flour
1 cup half-and-half or milk
1 teaspoon dried tarragon leaves
1 teaspoon salt
Black pepper
½ cup frozen peas
½ cup sour cream (optional)
Puff pastry shells (optional)

1. Layer turkey, onions and mushrooms in slow cooker. Cover and cook on LOW 4 hours. Remove turkey and vegetables to serving bowl. Turn slow cooker to HIGH.

2. Blend flour into half-and-half until smooth; pour into slow cooker. Add tarragon, salt and pepper to slow cooker. Return cooked vegetables and turkey to slow cooker. Stir in peas. Cover and cook 1 hour or until sauce has thickened and peas are heated through.

3. Stir in sour cream just before serving and serve over puff pastry shells, if desired. Garnish, if desired.

TIP **Freeze leftover stew in individual containers or resealable plastic food storage bags for quick dinners on busy weeknights.**

Turkey Mushroom Stew

Southwest Turkey Tenderloin Stew

Makes 6 servings

1 package (about 1½ pounds) turkey tenderloins, cut into ¾-inch pieces
1 tablespoon chili powder
1 teaspoon ground cumin
¼ teaspoon salt
1 medium red bell pepper, cut into ¾-inch pieces
1 medium green bell pepper, cut into ¾-inch pieces
¾ cup chopped red or yellow onion
3 cloves garlic, minced
1 can (15½ ounces) chili beans in spicy sauce, undrained
1 can (14½ ounces) chili-style stewed tomatoes, undrained
¾ cup prepared salsa or picante sauce
Fresh cilantro (optional)

Place turkey in slow cooker. Sprinkle chili powder, cumin and salt over turkey; toss to coat. Add bell peppers, onion, garlic, beans with sauce, tomatoes with juice, and salsa; mix well. Cover and cook on LOW 5 hours or until turkey is no longer pink in center and vegetables are crisp-tender. Ladle into bowls. Garnish with cilantro, if desired.

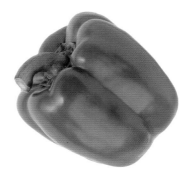

Southwest Turkey Tenderloin Stew

Panama Pork Stew

Makes 6 servings

**2 small sweet potatoes, peeled and cut into 2-inch pieces
(about 12 ounces total)**
1 package (10 ounces) frozen corn
1 package (9 ounces) frozen cut green beans
1 cup chopped onion
1¼ pounds lean pork stew meat, cut into 1-inch cubes
1 can (14½ ounces) diced tomatoes, undrained
1 cup water
1 to 2 tablespoons chili powder
½ teaspoon salt
½ teaspoon ground coriander

Place potatoes, corn, green beans and onion in slow cooker. Top with pork. Stir together tomatoes with juice, water, chili powder, salt and coriander in large bowl. Pour over pork in slow cooker. Cover and cook on LOW 7 to 9 hours. Garnish as desired.

Panama Pork Stew

Beef Stew with Molasses and Raisins

Makes 6 to 8 servings

⅓ cup all-purpose flour
2 teaspoons salt, divided
1½ teaspoons black pepper, divided
2 pounds boneless beef chuck roast, cut into 1½-inch
    cubes
5 tablespoons canola oil, divided
2 medium onions, sliced
1 can (28 ounces) diced tomatoes, drained
1 cup beef broth
3 tablespoons molasses
2 tablespoons cider vinegar
4 cloves garlic, minced
2 teaspoons dried thyme leaves
1 teaspoon celery salt
1 bay leaf
8 ounces baby carrots, cut lengthwise into halves
2 parsnips, diced
½ cup golden raisins
    Salt and black pepper

1. Combine flour, 1½ teaspoons salt and 1 teaspoon pepper in large bowl. Dredge beef cubes in flour mixture. Heat 2 tablespoons oil in large skillet over medium-high heat. Add half of beef and brown on all sides. Set aside browned beef and repeat with 2 tablespoons oil and remaining beef.

2. Add remaining 1 tablespoon oil to skillet. Add onions; cook, stirring to loosen any browned bits, about 5 minutes. Add tomatoes, broth, molasses, vinegar, garlic, thyme, celery salt, bay leaf and remaining ½ teaspoon salt and ½ teaspoon pepper. Bring to a boil. Add browned beef and boil 1 minute.

3. Transfer mixture to slow cooker. Cover and cook on LOW 5 hours or on HIGH 2½ hours. Add carrots, parsnips and raisins. Cook 1 to 2 hours or until vegetables are tender. Season with salt and pepper. Remove bay leaf before serving.

Bean Ragoût with Cilantro-Cornmeal Dumplings

Makes 6 servings

2 cans (14½ ounces each) tomatoes, chopped and juice reserved
1 can (15½ ounces) pinto or kidney beans, rinsed and drained
1 can (15½ ounces) black beans, rinsed and drained
1½ cups chopped red bell peppers
1 large onion, chopped
2 small zucchini, sliced
½ cup chopped green bell pepper
½ cup chopped celery
1 poblano chili pepper,* seeded and chopped
3 tablespoons chili powder
2 teaspoons ground cumin
2 cloves garlic, minced
1 teaspoon dried oregano leaves
¼ teaspoon salt
⅛ teaspoon black pepper
Cilantro-Cornmeal Dumplings (recipe on page 202)

Chili peppers can sting and irritate the skin; wear rubber gloves when handling peppers and do not touch eyes. Wash hands after handling.

Combine all ingredients except dumplings in slow cooker; mix well. Cover and cook on LOW 7 to 8 hours.

Continued on page 202

Bean Ragoût with Cilantro-Cornmeal Dumplings, *continued*

Cilantro-Cornmeal Dumplings

¼ cup all-purpose flour
¼ cup yellow cornmeal
½ teaspoon baking powder
¼ teaspoon salt
1 tablespoon vegetable shortening
2 tablespoons shredded Cheddar cheese
2 teaspoons minced fresh cilantro
¼ cup milk

Prepare dumplings 1 hour before serving. Mix flour, cornmeal, baking powder and salt in medium bowl. Cut in shortening with pastry blender or two knives until mixture resembles coarse crumbs. Stir in cheese and cilantro. Pour milk into flour mixture. Blend just until dry ingredients are moistened. Turn slow cooker to HIGH. Drop dumplings by level tablespoonfuls (larger dumplings will not cook properly) on top of ragoût. Cover and cook 1 hour or until toothpick inserted into dumpling comes out clean.

Bean Ragoût with Cilantro-Cornmeal Dumplings

Smoked Sausage Gumbo

Makes 4 servings

1 can (14½ ounces) diced tomatoes, undrained
1 cup chicken broth
¼ cup all-purpose flour
2 tablespoons olive oil
¾ pound Polish sausage, cut into ½-inch pieces
1 medium onion, diced
1 medium green bell pepper, diced
2 ribs celery, chopped
1 medium carrot, peeled and chopped
2 teaspoons dried oregano leaves
2 teaspoons dried thyme leaves
⅛ teaspoon ground red pepper
1 cup uncooked long-grain white rice

1. Combine tomatoes with juice and broth in slow cooker. Sprinkle flour evenly over bottom of small skillet. Cook over high heat, without stirring, 3 to 4 minutes or until flour begins to brown. Reduce heat to medium; stir flour about 4 minutes. Stir in oil until smooth. Carefully whisk flour mixture into slow cooker.

2. Add remaining ingredients except rice to slow cooker; stir well. Cover and cook on LOW 4½ to 5 hours or until juices are thickened.

3. About 30 minutes before gumbo is ready to serve, prepare rice. Cook rice in 2 cups boiling water in medium saucepan. Serve gumbo over rice.

Serving Suggestion: For a special touch, sprinkle chopped parsley over each serving.

Note: If gumbo thickens upon standing, stir in additional broth.

Smoked Sausage Gumbo

Garden Vegetable Tabbouleh Stew

Makes 4 servings

1 large onion, chopped
2 medium carrots, cut lengthwise into halves, then cut into 1-inch pieces
1 cup green beans, cut into 1-inch pieces
2 medium green onions, thinly sliced
1 small zucchini (4 ounces), sliced
1 can (15½ ounces) chick-peas (garbanzo beans), rinsed and drained
2 cans (14½ ounces each) diced tomatoes, undrained
¼ teaspoon salt
⅛ teaspoon black pepper
1 box (6 to 7 ounces) tabbouleh mix
1½ cups water
¼ cup olive oil
Sour cream (optional)
Fresh mint (optional)

Layer ingredients in slow cooker in the following order: onion, carrots, green beans, green onions, zucchini, chick-peas, tomatoes with juice, salt and pepper. Sprinkle tabbouleh mix over vegetables. Pour water and olive oil evenly over top. Cover and cook on LOW 6 to 8 hours or until vegetables are crisp-tender. Garnish with sour cream and fresh mint, if desired.

Black Bean and Sausage Stew

Makes 6 servings

3 cans (15 ounces each) black beans, rinsed and drained
1½ cups chopped onion
1½ cups fat-free reduced-sodium chicken broth
1 cup sliced celery
1 cup chopped red bell pepper
4 cloves garlic, minced
1½ teaspoons dried oregano leaves
¾ teaspoon ground coriander
½ teaspoon ground cumin
¼ teaspoon ground red pepper
6 ounces cooked turkey sausage, thinly sliced

1. Combine all ingredients except sausage in slow cooker. Cover and cook on LOW 6 to 8 hours.

2. Remove about 1½ cups bean mixture from slow cooker to blender or food processor; purée bean mixture. Return to slow cooker. Stir in sliced sausage. Cover and cook on LOW an additional 10 to 15 minutes.

Chicken Stew with Dumplings

Makes 4 servings

2 cups sliced carrots
1 cup chopped onion
1 large green bell pepper, sliced
½ cup sliced celery
2 cans (about 14 ounces each) chicken broth, divided
⅔ cup all-purpose flour
1 pound boneless skinless chicken breasts, cut into 1-inch pieces
1 large potato, unpeeled, cut into 1-inch pieces
6 ounces mushrooms, halved
¾ cup frozen peas
1 teaspoon dried basil leaves
¾ teaspoon dried rosemary leaves
¼ teaspoon dried tarragon leaves
¾ to 1 teaspoon salt
¼ teaspoon black pepper
¼ cup heavy cream

HERB DUMPLINGS
1 cup biscuit mix
¼ teaspoon dried basil leaves
¼ teaspoon dried rosemary leaves
⅛ teaspoon dried tarragon leaves
⅓ cup reduced-fat (2%) milk

1. Combine carrots, onion, green bell pepper and celery in slow cooker. Stir in chicken broth, reserving 1 cup broth. Cover and cook on LOW 2 hours.

2. Stir flour into remaining 1 cup broth until smooth; stir into slow cooker. Add chicken, potato, mushrooms, peas and herbs to slow cooker. Cover and cook 4 hours or until vegetables are tender and chicken is no longer pink. Stir in salt, black pepper and heavy cream.

3. For dumplings, combine biscuit mix and herbs in small bowl. Stir in milk to form soft dough. Spoon dumpling mixture on top of stew in 4 large spoonfuls. Cook, uncovered, 30 minutes. Cover and cook 30 to 45 minutes or until dumplings are firm and toothpick inserted into center of dumpling comes out clean. Serve in shallow bowls.

Chicken Stew with Dumplings

BEVERAGES & DESSERTS

Poached Pears with Raspberry Sauce

Makes 4 to 5 servings

4 cups cran-raspberry juice cocktail
2 cups Rhine or Riesling wine
¼ cup sugar
2 cinnamon sticks, broken into halves
4 to 5 firm Bosc or Anjou pears, peeled and cored
1 package (10 ounces) frozen raspberries in syrup, thawed
Fresh berries (optional)

1. Combine juice, wine, sugar and cinnamon stick halves in slow cooker. Submerge pears in mixture. Cover and cook on LOW 3½ to 4 hours or until pears are tender. Remove and discard cinnamon sticks.

2. Process raspberries in food processor or blender until smooth; strain out seeds. Spoon raspberry sauce onto serving plate; place pear on top of sauce. Garnish with fresh berries, if desired.

Coconut Rice Pudding

Makes 6 (¾-cup) servings

2 cups water
1 cup uncooked long-grain rice
1 tablespoon unsalted butter
Pinch salt
1½ cans (18 ounces) evaporated milk
14 ounces (about 1 can) cream of coconut
½ cup golden raisins
3 egg yolks, beaten
Zest of 2 limes
1 teaspoon vanilla

1. Bring water, rice, butter and salt to a rolling boil in medium saucepan, stirring frequently. Reduce heat to a simmer. Cover and cook 10 to 12 minutes. Remove from heat. Cover and set aside 5 minutes.

2. Meanwhile, spray slow cooker with nonstick cooking spray. Add remaining ingredients; mix well. Add rice mixture; stir. Cover and cook on LOW 4 hours or on HIGH 2 hours, stirring every 30 minutes. Pudding will thicken as it cools.

Poached Pears with Raspberry Sauce

English Bread Pudding

Makes 6 to 8 servings

16 slices day-old, firm-textured white bread (1 small loaf)
1¾ cups milk
1 package (8 ounces) mixed dried fruit, cut into small pieces
½ cup chopped nuts
1 medium apple, cored and chopped
⅓ cup packed brown sugar
¼ cup butter, melted
1 egg, slightly beaten
1 teaspoon ground cinnamon
¼ teaspoon ground nutmeg
¼ teaspoon ground cloves

1. Tear bread, with crusts, into 1- to 2-inch pieces. Place in slow cooker. Pour milk over bread; let soak 30 minutes. Stir in dried fruit, nuts and apple.

2. Combine remaining ingredients in small bowl. Pour over bread mixture; stir well to blend. Cover and cook on LOW 3½ to 4 hours or until toothpick inserted in center comes out clean.

TIP **Chopping dried fruits can be difficult. To make the job easier, cut them with kitchen scissors. Spray your scissors or chef's knife with nonstick cooking spray before cutting, so the fruit won't stick to the blade.**

English Bread Pudding

Decadent Chocolate Delight

Makes 12 servings

1 package chocolate cake mix
1 package (4-serving size) chocolate flavor instant pudding
**   and pie filling mix**
8 ounces sour cream
1 cup chocolate chips
1 cup water
4 eggs
¾ cup vegetable oil

Lightly grease inside of slow cooker. Combine all ingredients in large bowl.
Pour into slow cooker. Cover and cook on LOW 6 to 8 hours or on HIGH
3 to 4 hours. Serve hot or warm with ice cream.

Baked Ginger Apples

Makes 4 servings

4 large Red Delicious apples
8 tablespoons unsalted butter, melted
⅓ cup chopped macadamia nuts
¼ cup chopped dried apricots
2 tablespoons finely chopped crystallized ginger
1 tablespoon dark brown sugar
¾ cup brandy
½ cup vanilla instant pudding and pie filling mix
2 cups heavy cream

1. Slice tops off apples and core.

2. Combine melted butter, macadamia nuts, apricots, ginger and brown sugar
in small bowl. Fill cavities of apples with nut mixture. Place apples in slow
cooker. Pour in brandy. Cover and cook on LOW 4 hours or on HIGH 2 hours.

3. Gently remove apples from slow cooker. Set aside; keep warm. Whisk
together pudding mix and cream in small bowl. Add to slow cooker; combine
with brandy. Cover and cook on HIGH 30 minutes. Stir until smooth. Place
apples in slow cooker and keep warm until ready to serve.

Decadent Chocolate Delight

Luscious Pecan Bread Pudding

Makes 6 servings

    3 cups French bread cubes
    3 tablespoons chopped pecans, toasted
 2¼ cups low-fat (1%) milk
    ½ cup sugar
    2 eggs, beaten
    1 teaspoon vanilla
    ¾ teaspoon ground cinnamon, divided
    ¾ cup reduced-calorie cranberry juice cocktail
 1½ cups frozen pitted tart cherries
    2 tablespoons sugar substitute

1. Toss bread cubes and pecans in soufflé dish. Combine milk, sugar, eggs, vanilla and ½ teaspoon cinnamon in large bowl. Pour over bread mixture in soufflé dish. Cover tightly with foil. Make foil handles (see page 228). Place soufflé dish in slow cooker. Pour hot water into slow cooker to about 1½ inches from top of soufflé dish. Cover and cook on LOW 2 to 3 hours.

2. Meanwhile, stir together cranberry juice and remaining ¼ teaspoon cinnamon in small saucepan; stir in frozen cherries. Bring sauce to a boil over medium heat, about 5 minutes. Remove from heat. Stir in sugar substitute. Lift dish from slow cooker with foil handles. Serve with cherry sauce. Garnish as desired.

Cherry Rice Pudding

Makes 6 servings

 1½ cups milk
    1 cup hot cooked rice
    3 eggs, beaten
    ½ cup sugar
    ¼ cup dried cherries or cranberries
    ½ teaspoon almond extract
    ¼ teaspoon salt

Combine all ingredients in large bowl. Pour mixture into greased 1½-quart casserole. Cover with foil. Add rack to 5-quart slow cooker and pour in 1 cup water. Place casserole on rack. Cover and cook on LOW 4 to 5 hours. Remove casserole from slow cooker. Let stand 15 minutes before serving.

Luscious Pecan Bread Pudding

Banana-Rum Custard with Vanilla Wafers

Makes 5 servings

1½ cups milk
3 eggs
½ cup sugar
3 tablespoons dark rum or milk
⅛ teaspoon salt
1 medium banana, sliced ¼ inch thick
15 to 18 vanilla wafers
    Sliced strawberries, raspberries or kiwis, for garnish (optional)

1. Beat milk, eggs, sugar, rum and salt in medium bowl. Pour into 1-quart casserole. Do not cover.

2. Add rack to 5-quart slow cooker and pour in 1 cup water. Place casserole on rack. Cover and cook on LOW 3½ to 4 hours. Remove casserole from slow cooker. Arrange banana slices and wafers over custard. Garnish with strawberries, raspberries or kiwis, if desired.

Banana-Rum Custard with Vanilla Wafers

Spiced Apple & Cranberry Compote

Makes 6 servings

2½ **cups cranberry juice cocktail**
1 **package (6 ounces) dried apples**
½ **cup (2 ounces) dried cranberries**
½ **cup Rhine wine or apple juice**
½ **cup honey**
2 **cinnamon sticks, broken into halves**
    Frozen yogurt or ice cream (optional)
    Additional cinnamon sticks (optional)

Combine juice, apples, cranberries, wine, honey and cinnamon stick halves in slow cooker. Cover and cook on LOW 4 to 5 hours or until liquid is absorbed and fruit is tender. Remove and discard cinnamon stick halves. Ladle compote into bowls. Serve warm, at room temperature or chilled with scoop of frozen yogurt or ice cream. Garnish with additional cinnamon sticks, if desired.

Peach Cobbler

Makes 4 to 6 servings

2 **packages (16 ounces each) frozen peaches, thawed and
    drained**
¾ **cup plus one tablespoon sugar, divided**
2 **teaspoons ground cinnamon, divided**
½ **teaspoon ground nutmeg**
¾ **cup all-purpose flour**
6 **tablespoons butter, cut into bits**

Combine peaches with ¾ cup sugar, 1½ teaspoons cinnamon and nutmeg in medium bowl. Add peach mixture to slow cooker. For topping, combine flour, remaining 1 tablespoon sugar and ½ teaspoon cinnamon in separate medium bowl. Cut in butter with pastry cutter or two knives until mixture resembles coarse crumbs. Sprinkle over top of peach mixture in slow cooker. Cover and cook on HIGH 2 hours. Serve with freshly whipped cream, if desired.

Spiced Apple & Cranberry Compote

Mulled Wine

Makes 12 servings

**2 bottles (750 mL each) dry red wine, such as Cabernet
    Sauvignon**
1 cup light corn syrup
1 cup water
1 square (8 inches) double-thickness cheesecloth
Peel of 1 large orange
1 cinnamon stick, broken into halves
8 whole cloves
1 whole nutmeg

Combine wine, corn syrup and water in slow cooker. Rinse cheesecloth;
squeeze out water. Wrap orange peel, cinnamon stick halves, cloves and
nutmeg in cheesecloth. Tie securely with cotton string or strip of cheesecloth.
Add to slow cooker. Cover and cook on HIGH 2 to 2½ hours. Discard spice
bag; ladle wine into mugs. Garnish as desired.

Pumpkin Custard

Makes 6 servings

1 cup canned pumpkin
½ cup packed brown sugar
2 eggs, beaten
½ teaspoon ground ginger
½ teaspoon ground cinnamon
½ teaspoon grated lemon peel
1 can (12 ounces) evaporated milk
Additional ground cinnamon

1. Combine pumpkin, brown sugar, eggs, ginger, ½ teaspoon cinnamon and
lemon peel in large bowl. Stir in evaporated milk. Pour mixture into 1½-quart
soufflé dish. Cover tightly with foil.

2. Make foil handles (see page 228). Place soufflé dish in slow cooker. Pour
water into slow cooker to about 1½ inches from top of soufflé dish. Cover and
cook on LOW 4 hours. Use foil handles to lift dish from slow cooker. Sprinkle
with additional ground cinnamon. Serve warm.

Mulled Wine

Easy Chocolate Pudding Cake

Brandy Richardson ◆ *Tuscon, AZ*

Makes about 16 servings

**1 package (6-serving size) chocolate cook-and-serve
   pudding mix**
3 cups milk
**1 package (about 18 ounces) chocolate fudge cake mix and
   ingredients to prepare**
Whipped topping or ice cream (optional)

1. Spray inside of 4-quart slow cooker with nonstick cooking spray. Place
pudding mix in slow cooker. Whisk in milk.

2. Prepare cake mix in large bowl according to package directions. Carefully
pour cake mix into slow cooker. Do not stir. Cover and cook on HIGH
2½ hours or until cake is set. Serve warm with whipped topping or ice cream,
if desired.

Spiced Citrus Tea

Makes 6 servings

4 tea bags
Peel of 1 orange
4 cups boiling water
2 cans (6 ounces each) orange-pineapple juice
3 tablespoons honey
3 star anise
3 cinnamon sticks
Strawberries, raspberries or kiwis (optional)

1. Place tea bags and orange peel in slow cooker. Pour in boiling water. Cover
and let steep 10 minutes. Discard tea bags and orange peel.

2. Add remaining ingredients to slow cooker. Cover and cook on LOW
3 hours. Garnish with strawberries, raspberries or kiwis, if desired.

Pear Crunch

Makes 4 servings

1 can (8 ounces) crushed pineapple in juice, undrained
¼ cup pineapple juice or apple juice
3 tablespoons dried cranberries
1½ teaspoons quick-cooking tapioca
¼ teaspoon vanilla
2 large pears, cored and cut into halves
¼ cup granola with almonds

Combine all ingredients except pears and granola in slow cooker; mix well. Place pears, cut sides down, over pineapple mixture. Cover and cook on LOW 3½ to 4½ hours. Arrange pear halves on serving plates. Spoon pineapple mixture over pear halves. Garnish with granola.

Pumpkin-Cranberry Custard

Make 4 to 6 servings

1 can (30 ounces) pumpkin pie filling
1 can (12 ounces) evaporated milk
1 cup dried cranberries
4 eggs, beaten
1 cup crushed or whole ginger snap cookies (optional)
Whipped cream (optional)

Combine pumpkin, evaporated milk, cranberries and eggs in slow cooker and mix thoroughly. Cover and cook on HIGH 4 to 4½ hours. Serve with crushed or whole ginger snaps and whipped cream, if desired.

Fruit & Nut Baked Apples

Makes 4 servings

4 large baking apples, such as Rome Beauty or Jonathan
1 tablespoon lemon juice
⅓ cup chopped dried apricots
⅓ cup chopped walnuts or pecans
3 tablespoons packed brown sugar
½ teaspoon ground cinnamon
2 tablespoons melted butter or margarine

1. Scoop out center of each apple, leaving 1½-inch-wide cavity about ½ inch from bottom. Peel top of apple down about 1 inch. Brush peeled edges evenly with lemon juice. Mix apricots, walnuts, brown sugar and cinnamon in small bowl. Add butter; mix well. Spoon mixture evenly into apple cavities.

2. Pour ½ cup water into bottom of slow cooker. Place 2 apples in bottom of cooker. Arrange remaining 2 apples above, but not directly on top of, bottom apples. Cover and cook on LOW 3 to 4 hours or until apples are tender. Serve warm or at room temperature with caramel ice cream topping, if desired.

Note: Ever wonder why you need to brush lemon juice onto the peeled surface of an apple? Citrus fruits contain an acid that keeps apples, potatoes and other white vegetables from discoloring once they are cut or peeled.

Fruit & Nut Baked Apples

Steamed Southern Sweet Potato Custard

Makes 4 servings

1 can (16 ounces) cut sweet potatoes, drained
1 can (12 ounces) evaporated milk, divided
½ cup packed light brown sugar
2 eggs, lightly beaten
1 teaspoon ground cinnamon
½ teaspoon ground ginger
¼ teaspoon salt
   Whipped cream (optional)
   Ground nutmeg (optional)

1. Process sweet potatoes with about ¼ cup evaporated milk in food processor or blender until smooth. Add remaining milk, brown sugar, eggs, cinnamon, ginger and salt; process until well mixed. Pour into ungreased 1-quart soufflé dish. Cover tightly with foil.

2. Crumple large sheet (about 15×12 inches) of foil; place in bottom of slow cooker. Pour 2 cups water over foil. Make foil handles (see below); place soufflé dish on top of foil strips. Transfer dish to slow cooker, using foil handles; lay foil strips over top of dish. Cover and cook on HIGH 2½ to 3 hours or until skewer inserted in center comes out clean.

3. Using foil handles, lift dish from slow cooker and transfer to wire rack. Uncover; let stand 30 minutes. Garnish with whipped cream and nutmeg, if desired.

Foil Handles: To make foil handles, tear off three 18×3-inch strips of heavy-duty foil. Crisscross the strips so they resemble the spokes of a wheel. Place the dish or food in the center of the strips. Pull the foil strips up and over and place into the slow cooker. Leave them in while you cook, so you can easily lift the item out again when ready.

Steamed Southern Sweet Potato Custard

Triple Delicious Hot Chocolate

Makes 6 servings

⅓ **cup sugar**
¼ **cup unsweetened cocoa powder**
¼ **teaspoon salt**
3 **cups milk, divided**
¾ **teaspoon vanilla**
1 **cup heavy cream**
1 **square (1 ounce) bittersweet chocolate**
1 **square (1 ounce) white chocolate**
¾ **cup whipped cream**
2 **tablespoons mini chocolate chips or shaved bittersweet chocolate**

1. Combine sugar, cocoa, salt and ½ cup milk in medium bowl. Beat until smooth. Pour into slow cooker. Add remaining 2½ cups milk and vanilla. Cover and cook on LOW 2 hours.

2. Add cream. Cover and cook on LOW 10 minutes. Stir in bittersweet and white chocolates.

3. Pour hot chocolate into 6 coffee cups. Top each with 2 tablespoons whipped cream and 1 teaspoon chocolate chips.

"Peachy Keen" Dessert Treat

Makes 8 to 12 servings

1⅓ **cups uncooked old-fashioned oats**
1 **cup granulated sugar**
1 **cup packed light brown sugar**
⅔ **cup buttermilk baking mix**
2 **teaspoons ground cinnamon**
½ **teaspoon ground nutmeg**
2 **pounds fresh peaches (about 8 medium), sliced**

Stir together oats, sugars, baking mix, cinnamon and nutmeg in large bowl. Stir in peaches; mix until well blended. Pour mixture into slow cooker. Cover and cook on LOW 4 to 6 hours.

Triple Delicious Hot Chocolate

Chocolate Croissant Pudding

Makes 6 servings

1½ **cups milk**
3 **eggs**
½ **cup sugar**
¼ **cup unsweetened cocoa powder**
½ **teaspoon vanilla**
¼ **teaspoon salt**
2 **plain croissants, cut into 1-inch pieces**
½ **cup chocolate chips**
¾ **cup whipped cream (optional)**

1. Beat milk, eggs, sugar, cocoa, vanilla and salt in medium bowl.

2. Grease 1-quart casserole. Layer half the croissants, chocolate chips and half the egg mixture in casserole. Repeat layers with remaining croissants and egg mixture.

3. Add rack to 5-quart slow cooker; pour in 1 cup water. Place casserole on rack. Cover and cook on LOW 3 to 4 hours. Remove casserole from slow cooker. Top each serving with 2 tablespoons whipped cream, if desired.

Viennese Coffee

Makes about 4 servings

3 **cups strong freshly brewed hot coffee**
3 **tablespoons chocolate syrup**
1 **teaspoon sugar**
⅓ **cup heavy cream**
¼ **cup crème de cacao or Irish cream (optional)**
Whipped cream
Chocolate shavings for garnish

1. Combine coffee, chocolate syrup and sugar in slow cooker. Cover and cook on LOW 2 to 2½ hours. Stir in heavy cream and crème de cacao, if desired. Cover and cook 30 minutes or until heated through.

2. Ladle coffee into coffee cups; top with whipped cream and chocolate shavings.

Chocolate Croissant Pudding

DIPS, SAUCES & MORE

Caponata

Makes about 5¼ cups

- 1 medium eggplant (about 1 pound), peeled and cut into ½-inch pieces
- 1 can (14½ ounces) diced Italian plum tomatoes, undrained
- 1 medium onion, chopped
- 1 medium red bell pepper, cut into ½-inch pieces
- ½ cup prepared medium-hot salsa
- ¼ cup extra-virgin olive oil
- 2 tablespoons capers, drained
- 2 tablespoons balsamic vinegar
- 3 cloves garlic, minced
- 1 teaspoon dried oregano leaves
- ¼ teaspoon salt
- ⅓ cup packed fresh basil leaves, cut into thin strips
- Toasted sliced Italian or French bread

Combine all ingredients except basil and bread in slow cooker. Cover and cook on LOW 7 to 8 hours or until vegetables are crisp-tender. Stir in basil. Serve at room temperature on toasted bread.

Red Pepper Relish

Makes 4 servings

- 2 large red bell peppers, cut into thin strips
- 1 small Vidalia or other sweet onion, thinly sliced
- 3 tablespoons cider vinegar
- 2 tablespoons packed light brown sugar
- 1 tablespoon vegetable oil
- 1 tablespoon honey
- ¼ teaspoon salt
- ¼ teaspoon dried thyme leaves
- ¼ teaspoon red pepper flakes
- ¼ teaspoon black pepper

Combine all ingredients in slow cooker; mix well. Cover and cook on LOW 4 hours.

Caponata

Broccoli & Cheese Strata

Makes 4 servings

2 cups chopped broccoli florets
4 slices firm white bread, ½ inch thick
4 teaspoons butter
1½ cups (6 ounces) shredded Cheddar cheese
1½ cups low-fat (1%) milk
3 eggs
½ teaspoon salt
½ teaspoon hot pepper sauce
⅛ teaspoon black pepper

1. Cook broccoli in boiling water 10 minutes or until tender; drain. Spread one side of each bread slice with 1 teaspoon butter.

2. Arrange 2 slices bread, buttered sides up, in greased 1-quart casserole that will fit in slow cooker. Layer cheese, broccoli and remaining 2 bread slices, buttered sides down.

3. Beat together milk, eggs, salt, hot pepper sauce and pepper in medium bowl. Gradually pour over bread.

4. Place small wire rack in 5-quart slow cooker. Pour in 1 cup water. Place casserole on rack. Cover and cook on HIGH 3 hours.

Broccoli & Cheese Strata

Lamb in Dill Sauce

Makes 6 servings

2 large boiling potatoes, peeled and cut into 1-inch cubes
½ cup chopped onion
1½ teaspoons salt
½ teaspoon black pepper
½ teaspoon dried dill weed *or* 4 sprigs fresh dill
1 bay leaf
2 pounds lean lamb stew meat, cut into 1-inch cubes
1 cup plus 3 tablespoons water, divided
2 tablespoons all-purpose flour
1 teaspoon sugar
2 tablespoons lemon juice
Fresh dill (optional)

1. Layer ingredients in slow cooker in the following order: potatoes, onion, salt, pepper, dill, bay leaf, lamb and 1 cup water. Cover and cook on LOW 6 to 8 hours.

2. Remove lamb and potatoes with slotted spoon; cover and keep warm. Remove and discard bay leaf. Turn heat to HIGH.

3. Stir flour and remaining 3 tablespoons water in small bowl until smooth. Add half of cooking juices and sugar. Mix well and return to slow cooker. Cover and cook 15 minutes. Stir in lemon juice.

4. Return lamb and potatoes to slow cooker. Cover and cook 10 minutes or until heated through. Garnish with fresh dill, if desired.

Lamb in Dill Sauce

Chili con Queso

Makes 3 cups

1 pound pasteurized process cheese spread, cut into cubes
1 can (10 ounces) diced tomatoes and green chilies,
**   undrained**
1 cup sliced green onions
2 teaspoons ground coriander
2 teaspoons ground cumin
¾ teaspoon hot pepper sauce
**   Green onion strips (optional)**
**   Hot pepper slices (optional)**

Combine all ingredients except green onion strips and hot pepper slices in slow cooker until well blended. Cover and cook on LOW 2 to 3 hours or until hot.* Garnish with green onion strips and hot pepper slices, if desired.

Chili will be very hot; use caution when serving.

Serving Suggestion: Serve Chili con Queso with tortilla chips. Or, for something different, cut pita bread into triangles and toast in preheated 400°F oven 5 minutes or until crisp.

Curried Snack Mix

Makes 16 servings

3 tablespoons butter
2 tablespoons brown sugar
1½ teaspoons hot curry powder
¼ teaspoon salt
¼ teaspoon ground cumin
2 cups rice squares cereal
1 cup walnut halves
1 cup dried cranberries

Melt butter in large skillet. Add brown sugar, curry powder, salt and cumin; mix well. Add cereal, walnuts and cranberries; stir to coat. Spoon mixture into slow cooker. Cover and cook on LOW 3 hours. Remove cover; cook additional 30 minutes.

Chili con Queso

Mom's Tuna Casserole

Makes 8 servings

2 cans (12 ounces each) tuna, drained and flaked
3 cups diced celery
3 cups crushed potato chips, divided
6 hard-cooked eggs, chopped
1 can (10¾ ounces) condensed cream of mushroom soup,
**   undiluted**
1 can (10¾ ounces) condensed cream of celery soup,
**   undiluted**
1 cup mayonnaise
1 teaspoon dried tarragon leaves
1 teaspoon black pepper

Combine all ingredients except ½ cup potato chips in slow cooker; stir well.
Top mixture with remaining ½ cup potato chips. Cover and cook on LOW
5 to 8 hours.

Meatless Sloppy Joes

Makes 4 servings

2 cups thinly sliced onions
2 cups chopped green peppers
1 can (about 15 ounces) kidney beans, rinsed, drained and
**   mashed**
1 can (8 ounces) tomato sauce
2 tablespoons ketchup
1 tablespoon mustard
2 cloves garlic, finely chopped
1 teaspoon chili powder
** Cider vinegar (optional)**
2 sandwich rolls, halved

Spray inside of slow cooker with nonstick cooking spray. Combine all
ingredients except rolls in slow cooker. Cover and cook on LOW 5 to
5½ hours or until vegetables are tender. Serve on rolls.

Mom's Tuna Casserole

Festive Bacon & Cheese Dip

Makes about 1 quart

**2 packages (8 ounces each) cream cheese, softened and cut
    into cubes
4 cups shredded Colby-Jack cheese
1 cup half-and-half
2 tablespoons mustard
1 tablespoon chopped onion
2 teaspoons Worcestershire sauce
½ teaspoon salt
¼ teaspoon hot pepper sauce
1 pound bacon, cooked and crumbled**

Combine cream cheese, Colby-Jack cheese, half-and-half, mustard, onion,
Worcestershire, salt and pepper sauce in slow cooker. Cover and cook on
LOW 1 hour, stirring occasionally, or until cheese melts. Stir in bacon; adjust
seasonings as desired. Serve with crusty bread or fruit and vegetable dippers.

Onion Marmalade

Makes 5 cups

**1 (12-ounce) bottle balsamic vinegar (1½ cups)
1 (12-ounce) bottle white wine vinegar (1½ cups)
1½ cups dark brown sugar
3 tablespoons arrowroot or cornstarch dissolved in
    2 tablespoons water
2 teaspoons cumin seeds
2 teaspoons coriander seeds
4 large yellow onions, sliced into halves, then into ¼-inch
    slices**

1. With exhaust fan running, cook vinegars in large saucepan over high heat
until reduced to ¼ cup. Sauce will be thick and syrupy. Remove from heat.
Add brown sugar, arrowroot mixture, cumin and coriander. Blend well.

2. Place onions in slow cooker. Add balsamic syrup mixture; mix well. Cover
and cook on LOW 8 to 10 hours or on HIGH 4 to 6 hours or until onions are
no longer crunchy. Stir frequently. Will keep in refrigerator several weeks.

Festive Bacon & Cheese Dip

Garden Potato Casserole

Makes 5 servings

1¼ pounds baking potatoes, unpeeled, sliced
1 small red or green bell pepper, thinly sliced
¼ cup finely chopped yellow onion
½ teaspoon salt
½ teaspoon dried thyme leaves
Black pepper
2 tablespoons butter, cut into ⅛-inch pieces, divided
1 small yellow squash, thinly sliced
1 cup (4 ounces) shredded sharp Cheddar cheese

1. Combine potatoes, bell pepper, onion, salt, thyme, black pepper and 1 tablespoon butter in slow cooker; mix well. Layer squash evenly over all and sprinkle with remaining 1 tablespoon butter. Cover and cook on LOW 7 hours or on HIGH 4 hours.

2. Remove potato mixture to serving platter. Sprinkle with cheese and let stand 2 to 3 minutes or until cheese melts.

Garden Potato Casserole

Do you have your own favorite recipes? We'd love to hear about them! Send them in, along with the submission forms below. Your recipes could be chosen for one of our upcoming cookbooks!

HOME-TESTED
RECIPES
pil

SUBMISSION FORM

Please attach to your recipe

Name:_____

Address:_____

City:_____ **State:**____ **Zip:**_____

Phone:_____ **Email:**_____

Recipe Name:_____

Category (Check One): ❑ **Slow Cooker**   ❑ **Desserts**
                          ❑ **Casseroles**   ❑ **Cookies**

Mail to: Home-Tested Recipes, Cookbook Dept., Publications
International, Ltd., 7373 N. Cicero Ave., Lincolnwood, IL 60712

HOME-TESTED
RECIPES
pil

SUBMISSION FORM

Please attach to your recipe

Name:_____

Address:_____

City:_____ **State:**____ **Zip:**_____

Phone:_____ **Email:**_____

Recipe Name:_____

Category (Check One): ❑ **Slow Cooker**   ❑ **Desserts**
                          ❑ **Casseroles**   ❑ **Cookies**

Mail to: Home-Tested Recipes, Cookbook Dept., Publications
International, Ltd., 7373 N. Cicero Ave., Lincolnwood, IL 60712

METRIC CONVERSION CHART

VOLUME MEASUREMENTS (dry)

$1/8$ teaspoon = 0.5 mL
$1/4$ teaspoon = 1 mL
$1/2$ teaspoon = 2 mL
$3/4$ teaspoon = 4 mL
1 teaspoon = 5 mL
1 tablespoon = 15 mL
2 tablespoons = 30 mL
$1/4$ cup = 60 mL
$1/3$ cup = 75 mL
$1/2$ cup = 125 mL
$2/3$ cup = 150 mL
$3/4$ cup = 175 mL
1 cup = 250 mL
2 cups = 1 pint = 500 mL
3 cups = 750 mL
4 cups = 1 quart = 1 L

VOLUME MEASUREMENTS (fluid)

1 fluid ounce (2 tablespoons) = 30 mL
4 fluid ounces ($1/2$ cup) = 125 mL
8 fluid ounces (1 cup) = 250 mL
12 fluid ounces ($1 1/2$ cups) = 375 mL
16 fluid ounces (2 cups) = 500 mL

WEIGHTS (mass)

$1/2$ ounce = 15 g
1 ounce = 30 g
3 ounces = 90 g
4 ounces = 120 g
8 ounces = 225 g
10 ounces = 285 g
12 ounces = 360 g
16 ounces = 1 pound = 450 g

DIMENSIONS

$1/16$ inch = 2 mm
$1/8$ inch = 3 mm
$1/4$ inch = 6 mm
$1/2$ inch = 1.5 cm
$3/4$ inch = 2 cm
1 inch = 2.5 cm

OVEN TEMPERATURES

250°F = 120°C
275°F = 140°C
300°F = 150°C
325°F = 160°C
350°F = 180°C
375°F = 190°C
400°F = 200°C
425°F = 220°C
450°F = 230°C

BAKING PAN SIZES

Utensil	Size in Inches/Quarts	Metric Volume	Size in Centimeters
Baking or Cake Pan (square or rectangular)	$8 \times 8 \times 2$	2 L	$20 \times 20 \times 5$
	$9 \times 9 \times 2$	2.5 L	$23 \times 23 \times 5$
	$12 \times 8 \times 2$	3 L	$30 \times 20 \times 5$
	$13 \times 9 \times 2$	3.5 L	$33 \times 23 \times 5$
Loaf Pan	$8 \times 4 \times 3$	1.5 L	$20 \times 10 \times 7$
	$9 \times 5 \times 3$	2 L	$23 \times 13 \times 7$
Round Layer Cake Pan	$8 \times 1 1/2$	1.2 L	20×4
	$9 \times 1 1/2$	1.5 L	23×4
Pie Plate	$8 \times 1 1/4$	750 mL	20×3
	$9 \times 1 1/4$	1 L	23×3
Baking Dish or Casserole	1 quart	1 L	—
	$1 1/2$ quart	1.5 L	—
	2 quart	2 L	—